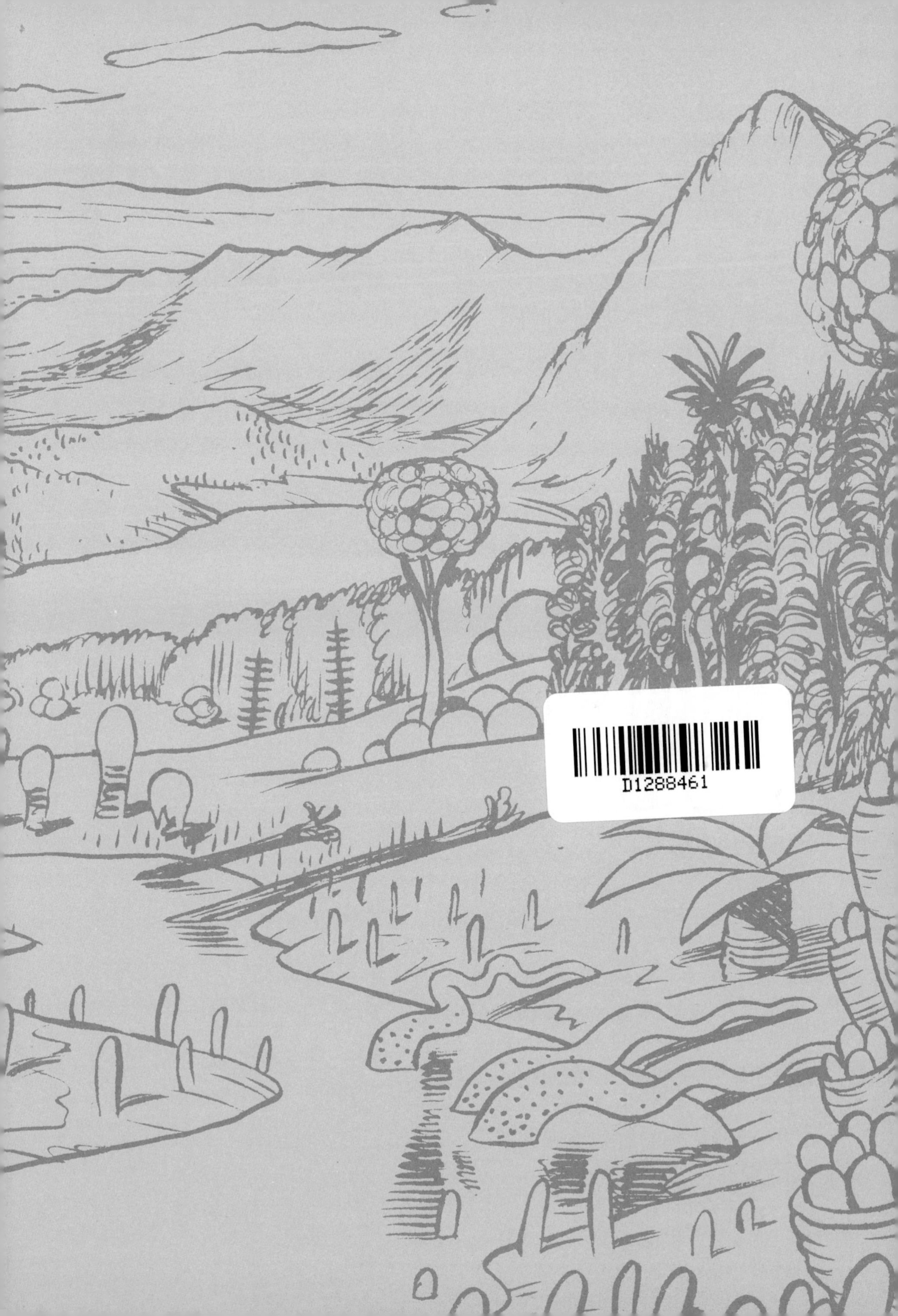

Frederik Peeters

2. The Invisible Throng

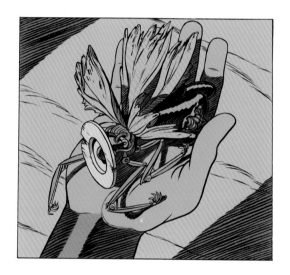

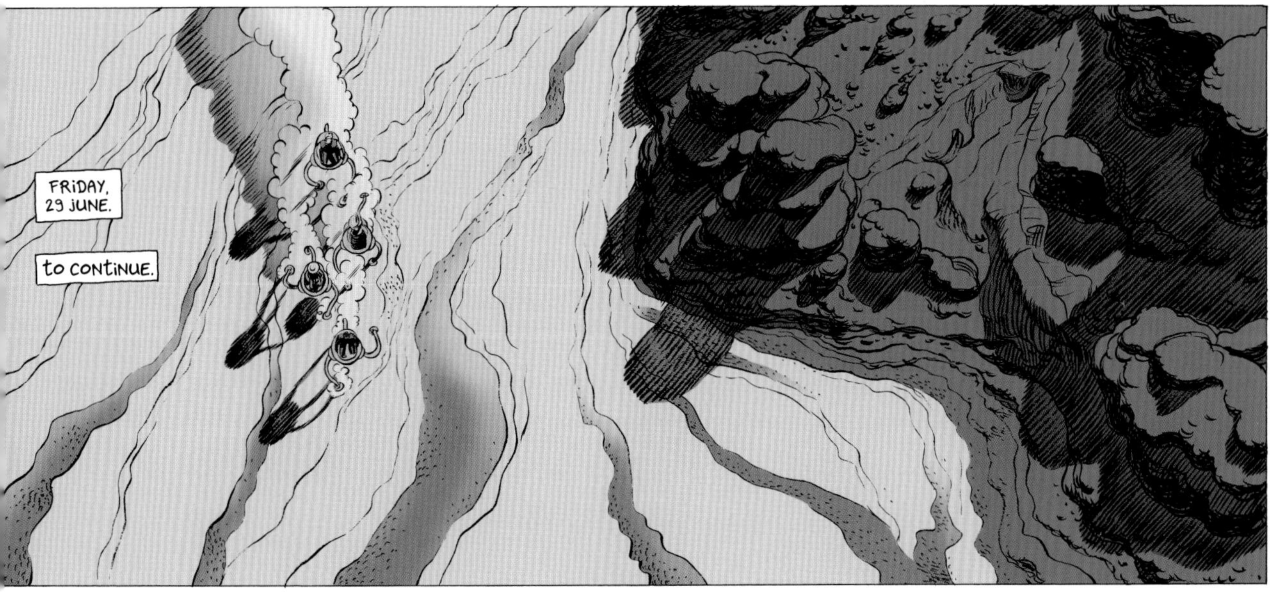
FRIDAY, 29 JUNE.
to CONTINUE.

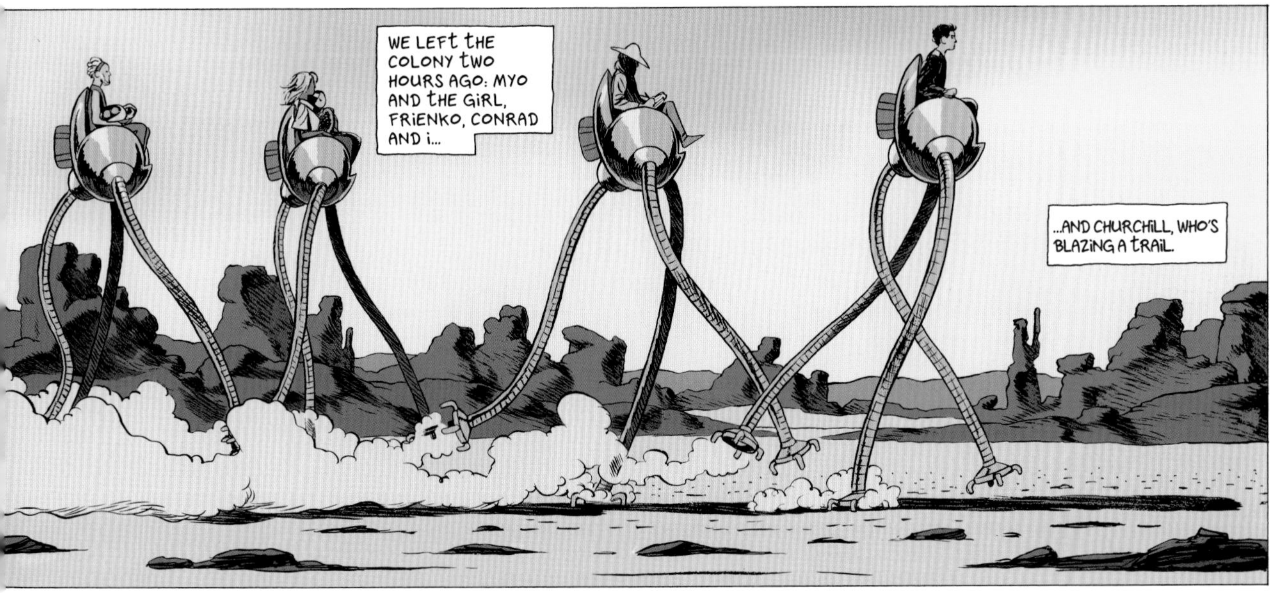
WE LEFT THE COLONY TWO HOURS AGO: MYO AND THE GIRL, FRIENKO, CONRAD AND I...
...AND CHURCHILL, WHO'S BLAZING A TRAIL.

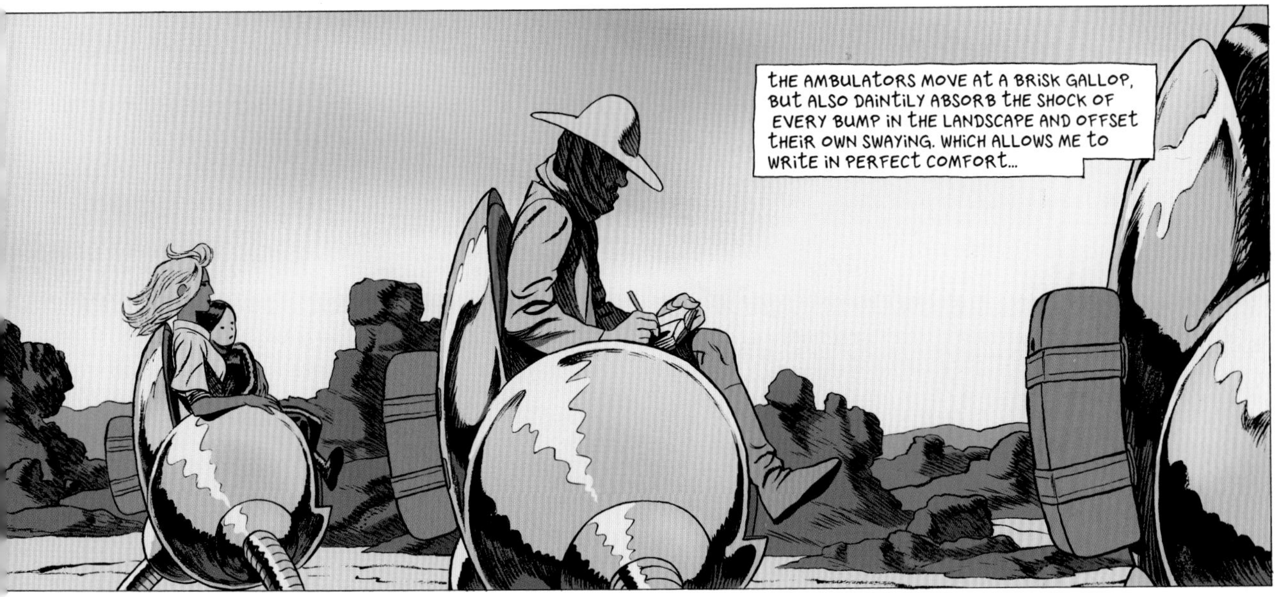
THE AMBULATORS MOVE AT A BRISK GALLOP, BUT ALSO DAINTILY ABSORB THE SHOCK OF EVERY BUMP IN THE LANDSCAPE AND OFFSET THEIR OWN SWAYING. WHICH ALLOWS ME TO WRITE IN PERFECT COMFORT...

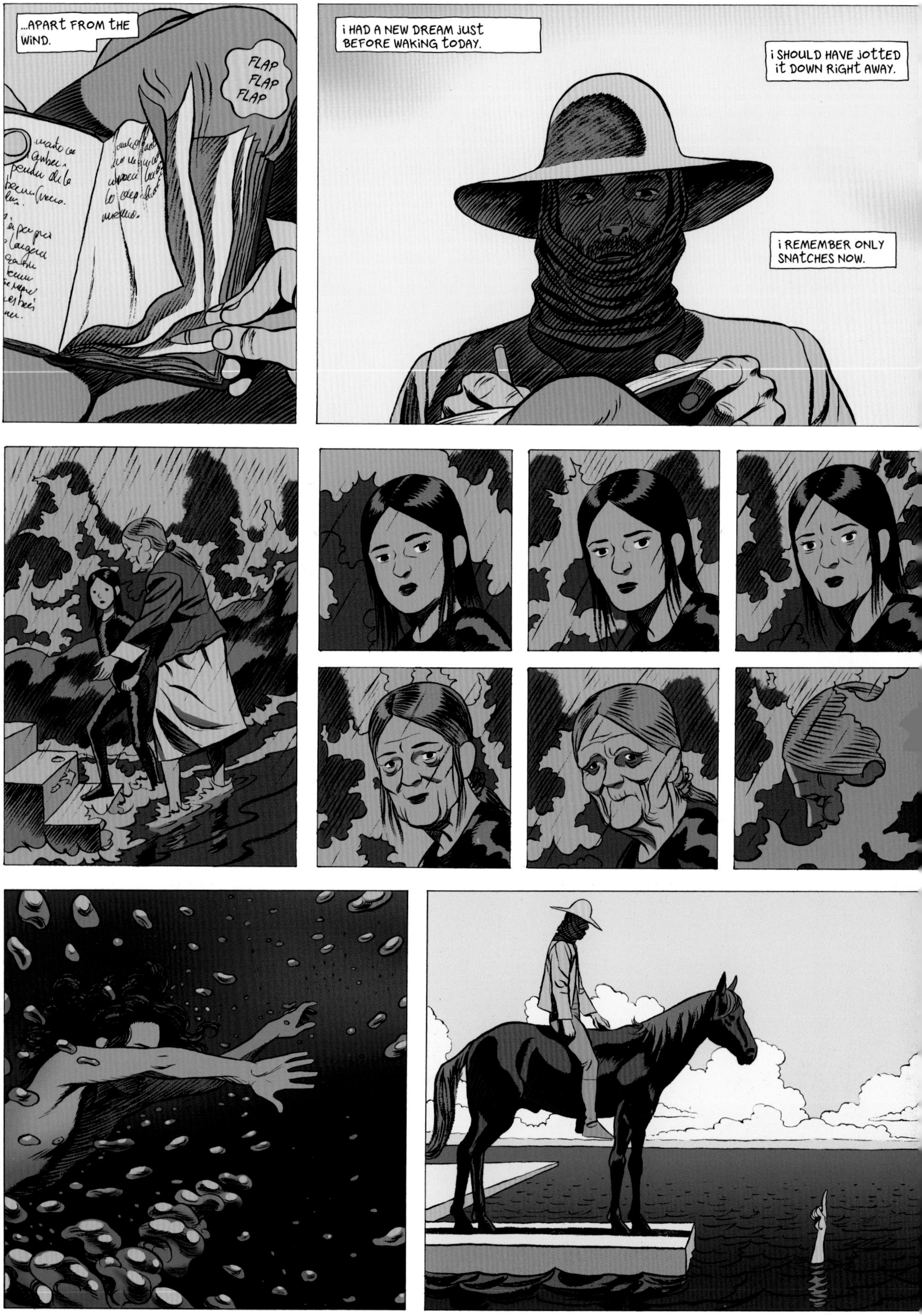
...APART FROM THE WIND.
FLAP FLAP FLAP
I HAD A NEW DREAM JUST BEFORE WAKING TODAY.
I SHOULD HAVE JOTTED IT DOWN RIGHT AWAY.
I REMEMBER ONLY SNATCHES NOW.

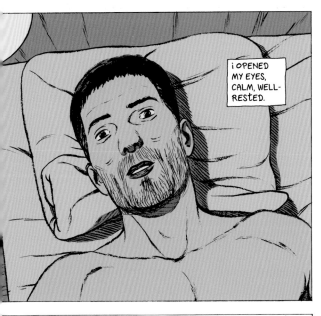

i OPENED MY EYES, CALM, WELL-RESTED.
SO MUCH SO that i STAYED iN BED A FEW LONG MiNUtES, WAtCHiNG EYE FLOATERS WANDER AGAiNSt tHE CEiLiNG'S BACKDROP.
LACKiNG A SAtiSFYiNG EXPLANAtiON FOR tHEM, i'VE ALWAYS LiKED tO iMAGiNE tHEM AS tiNY CREAtURES iNHABiTiNG MY OCULAR FLUiDS. it'S BEEN A LONG tiME SiNCE i CONtEMPLAtED tHEM. tHEY CAME BACK WHEN i GOt MY iMPLANtS tAKEN OUt.
APPARENtLY tHEY'RE LiNKED tO SEVERE MYOPiA. AS iF tHE EYE, tiRED OR DiSAPPOiNtED FROM SCANNiNG tHE BLURRY WORLD OUtSiDE, DECiDED tO tAKE A BREAK AND tURN itS GAZE iNWARD.
SSSSSSSSSS
But SOON REALity CAUGHt UP WiTH ME.
SNiFF

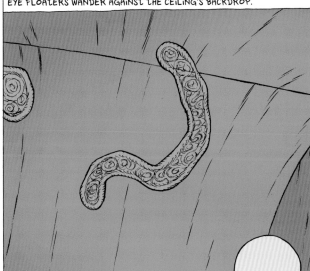

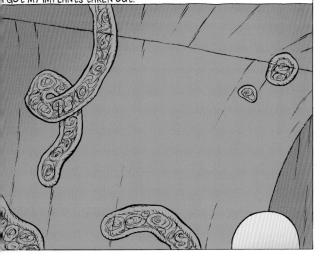

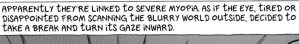

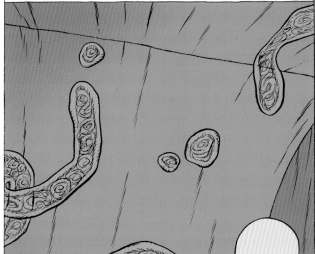

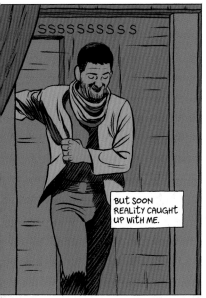

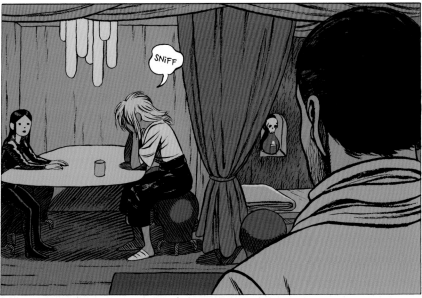

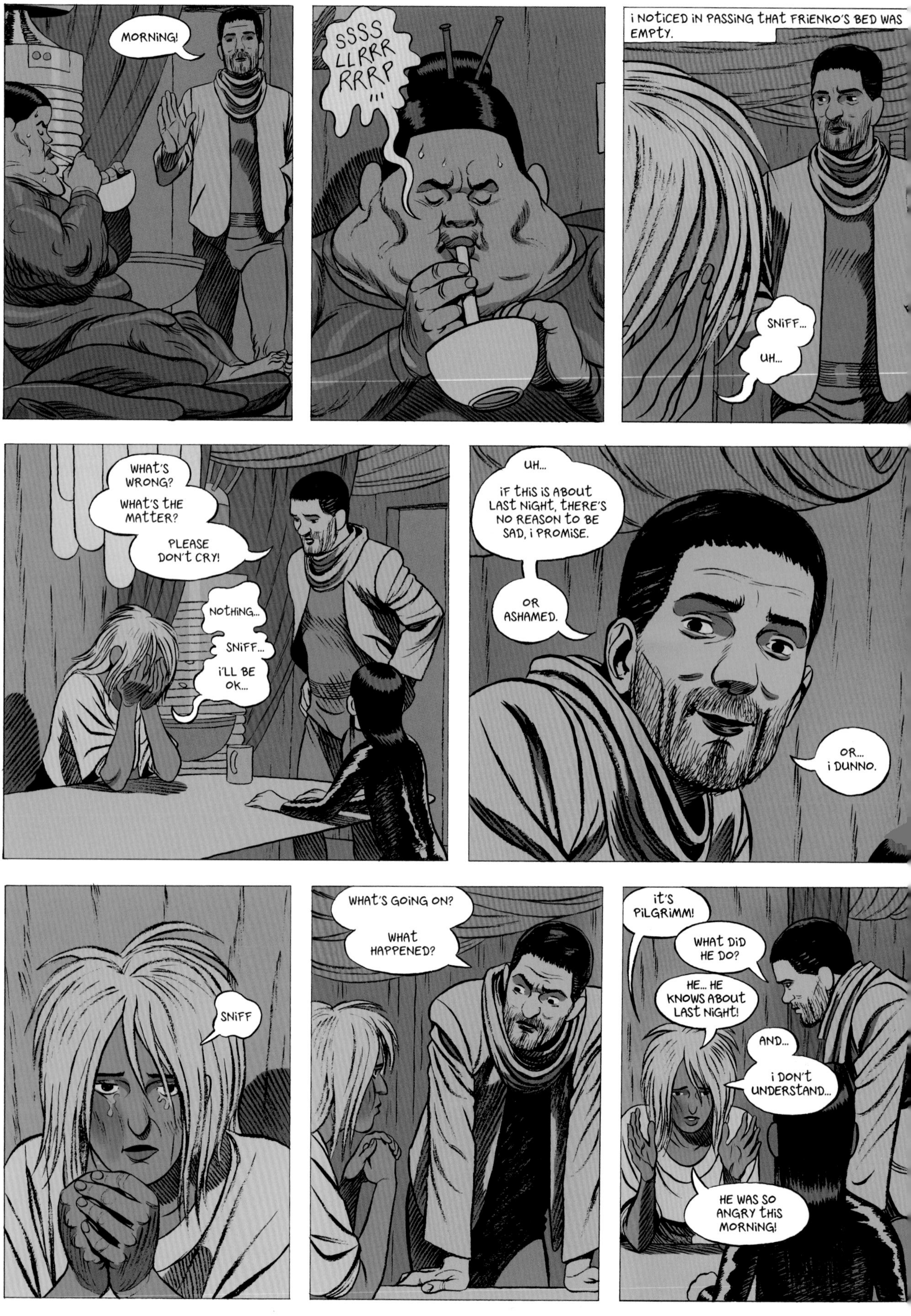
MORNING!
SSSS LLRRR RRRP !!!
i NOTICED IN PASSING THAT FRIENKO'S BED WAS EMPTY.
SNiFF...
UH...
WHAT'S WRONG?
WHAT'S THE MATTER?
PLEASE DON'T CRY!
NOTHING...
SNiFF...
i'LL BE OK...
UH...
iF THIS IS ABOUT LAST NiGHT, THERE'S NO REASON TO BE SAD, i PROMiSE.
OR ASHAMED.
OR... i DUNNO.
SNiFF
WHAT'S GOiNG ON?
WHAT HAPPENED?
iT'S PiLGRiMM!
WHAT DiD HE DO?
HE... HE KNOWS ABOUT LAST NiGHT!
AND...
i DON'T UNDERSTAND...
HE WAS SO ANGRY THiS MORNiNG!

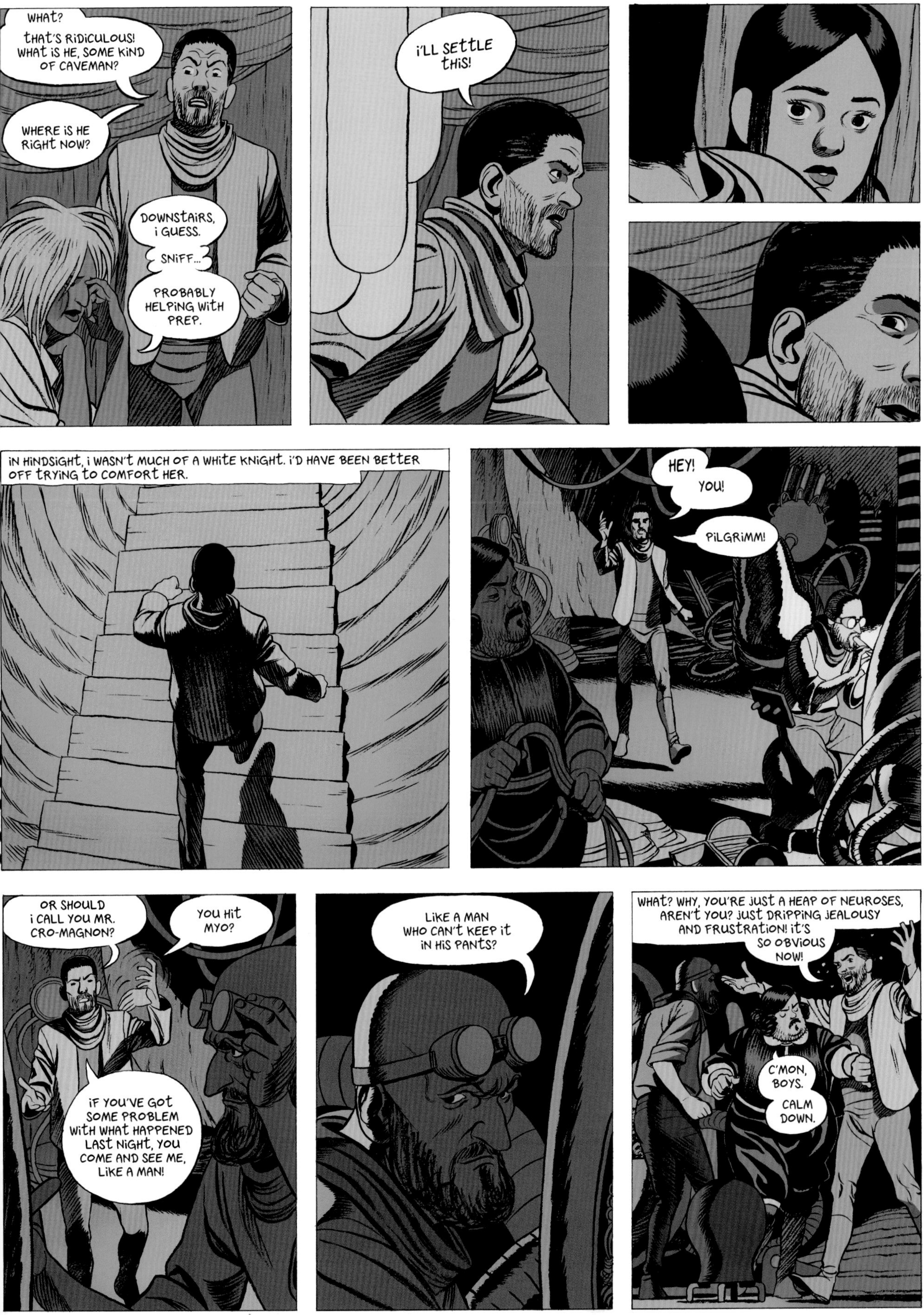
WHAT?
THAT'S RIDICULOUS! WHAT IS HE, SOME KIND OF CAVEMAN?
WHERE IS HE RIGHT NOW?
DOWNSTAIRS, I GUESS.
SNIFF...
PROBABLY HELPING WITH PREP.
I'LL SETTLE THIS!
IN HINDSIGHT, I WASN'T MUCH OF A WHITE KNIGHT. I'D HAVE BEEN BETTER OFF TRYING TO COMFORT HER.
HEY!
YOU!
PILGRIMM!
OR SHOULD I CALL YOU MR. CRO-MAGNON?
YOU HIT MYO?
IF YOU'VE GOT SOME PROBLEM WITH WHAT HAPPENED LAST NIGHT, YOU COME AND SEE ME, LIKE A MAN!
LIKE A MAN WHO CAN'T KEEP IT IN HIS PANTS?
WHAT? WHY, YOU'RE JUST A HEAP OF NEUROSES, AREN'T YOU? JUST DRIPPING JEALOUSY AND FRUSTRATION! IT'S SO OBVIOUS NOW!
C'MON, BOYS.
CALM DOWN.

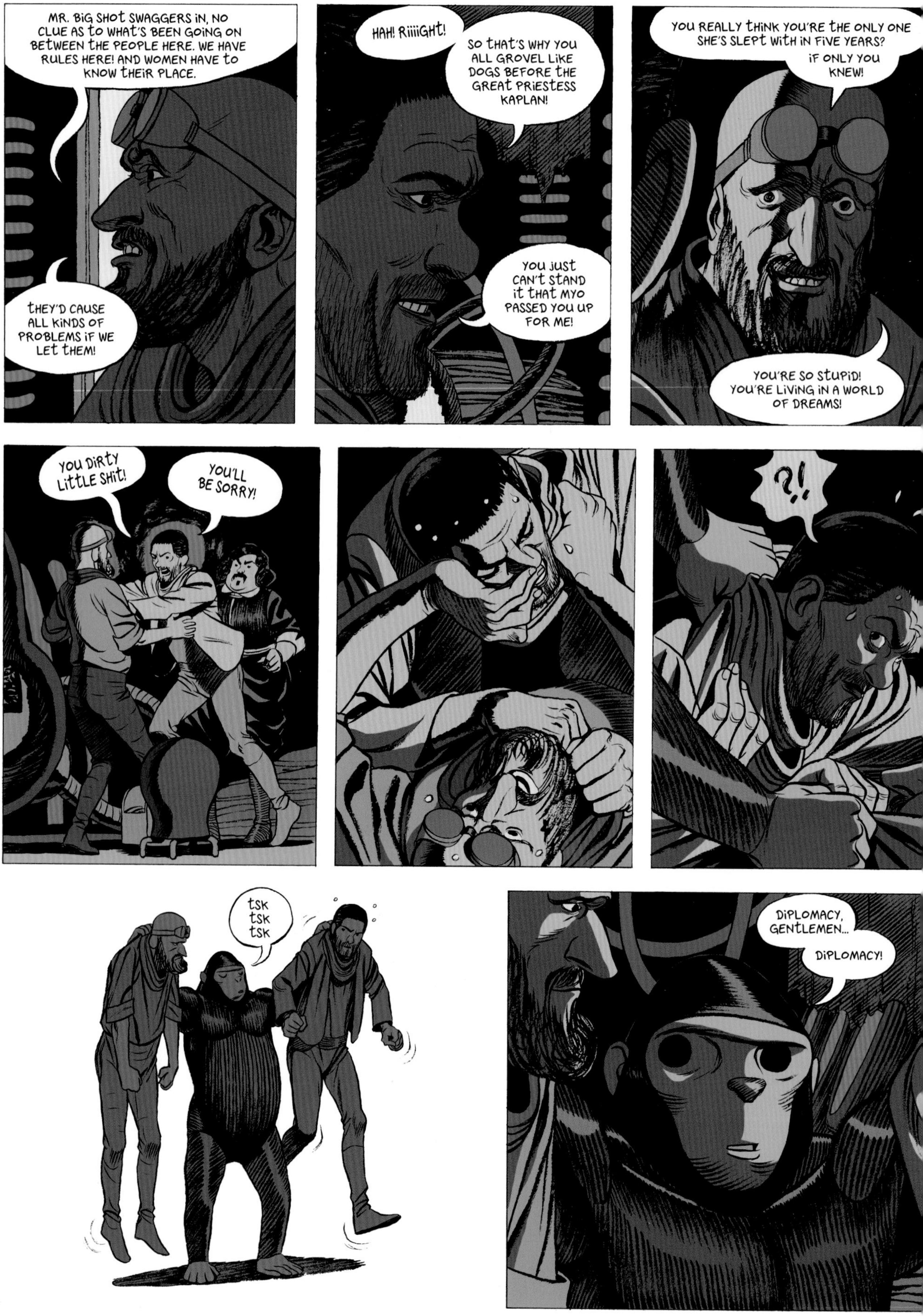
MR. BIG SHOT SWAGGERS IN, NO CLUE AS TO WHAT'S BEEN GOING ON BETWEEN THE PEOPLE HERE. WE HAVE RULES HERE! AND WOMEN HAVE TO KNOW THEIR PLACE.
THEY'D CAUSE ALL KINDS OF PROBLEMS IF WE LET THEM!
HAH! RIIIIGHT!
SO THAT'S WHY YOU ALL GROVEL LIKE DOGS BEFORE THE GREAT PRIESTESS KAPLAN!
YOU JUST CAN'T STAND IT THAT MYO PASSED YOU UP FOR ME!
YOU REALLY THINK YOU'RE THE ONLY ONE SHE'S SLEPT WITH IN FIVE YEARS?
IF ONLY YOU KNEW!
YOU'RE SO STUPID! YOU'RE LIVING IN A WORLD OF DREAMS!
YOU DIRTY LITTLE SHIT!
YOU'LL BE SORRY!
?!
TSK TSK TSK
DIPLOMACY, GENTLEMEN...
DIPLOMACY!

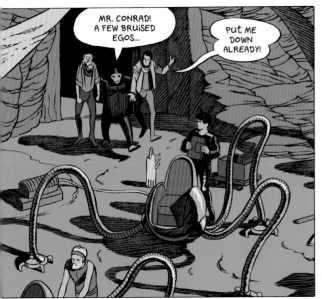

MR. CONRAD! A FEW BRUISED EGOS...

PUT ME DOWN ALREADY!

WHAT ARE YOU DOING, VERLOC? WE'RE NOT HERE TO POLICE PEOPLE.

BUT THIS BASTARD HIT MYO!

DO I HAVE TO SAY IT?

I COULDN'T GIVE LESS OF A SHIT!

WHY'D YOU SLEEP WITH HER, ANYWAY?

AH. SO YOU'VE HEARD.

SIGH

CHURCHILL! PUT 'EM DOWN.

OF COURSE I'VE HEARD.

EVERYONE HEARD THEM SHOUTING AT EACH OTHER THIS MORNING, WHILE YOU WERE SLEEPING IN.

LOOK, THESE PEOPLE FORMED THEIR OWN LITTLE MICROCOSM TO SURVIVE ISOLATION. YOU SHOULD'VE REALIZED THIS WOULD FUCK THINGS UP.

YOU THINK IT'S OK THAT SOME REPRESSED LITTLE SHIT SHOULD TAKE IT OUT ON A WOMAN?

I'M NOT TAKING SIDES. I'M NOT HERE TO BE THEIR SOCIAL WORKER. MY MISSION'S IN A TAILSPIN, I DON'T HAVE TIME FOR DISTRACTIONS.

YOUR MISSION! OF COURSE! LITTLE TIN SOLDIER!

COME HERE, WE HAVE TO TALK.

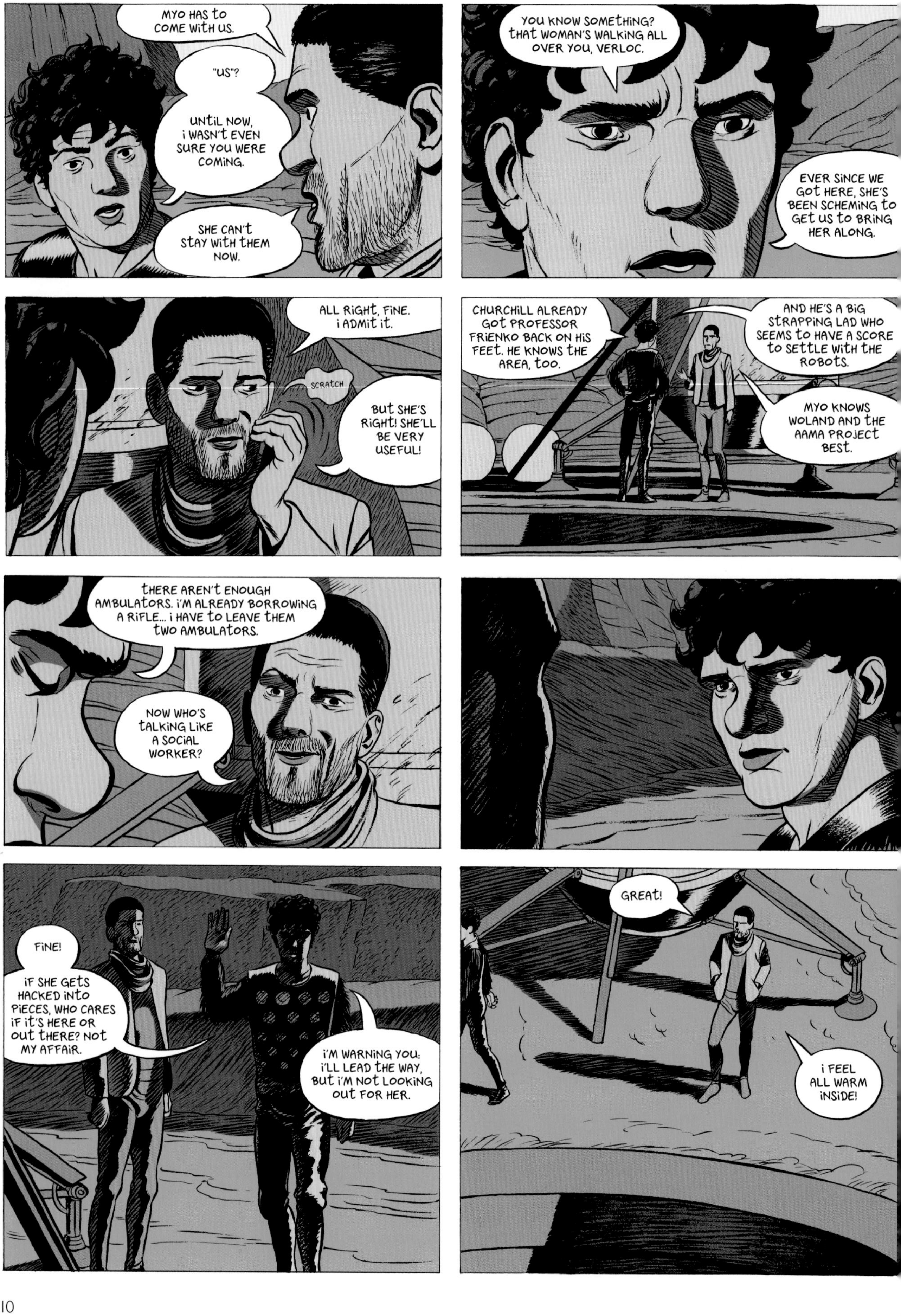
MYO HAS TO COME WITH US.
"US"?
UNTIL NOW, I WASN'T EVEN SURE YOU WERE COMING.
SHE CAN'T STAY WITH THEM NOW.
YOU KNOW SOMETHING? THAT WOMAN'S WALKING ALL OVER YOU, VERLOC.
EVER SINCE WE GOT HERE, SHE'S BEEN SCHEMING TO GET US TO BRING HER ALONG.
ALL RIGHT, FINE. I ADMIT IT.
SCRATCH
BUT SHE'S RIGHT! SHE'LL BE VERY USEFUL!
CHURCHILL ALREADY GOT PROFESSOR FRIENKO BACK ON HIS FEET. HE KNOWS THE AREA, TOO.
AND HE'S A BIG STRAPPING LAD WHO SEEMS TO HAVE A SCORE TO SETTLE WITH THE ROBOTS.
MYO KNOWS WOLAND AND THE AAMA PROJECT BEST.
THERE AREN'T ENOUGH AMBULATORS. I'M ALREADY BORROWING A RIFLE... I HAVE TO LEAVE THEM TWO AMBULATORS.
NOW WHO'S TALKING LIKE A SOCIAL WORKER?
FINE!
IF SHE GETS HACKED INTO PIECES, WHO CARES IF IT'S HERE OR OUT THERE? NOT MY AFFAIR.
I'M WARNING YOU: I'LL LEAD THE WAY, BUT I'M NOT LOOKING OUT FOR HER.
GREAT!
I FEEL ALL WARM INSIDE!

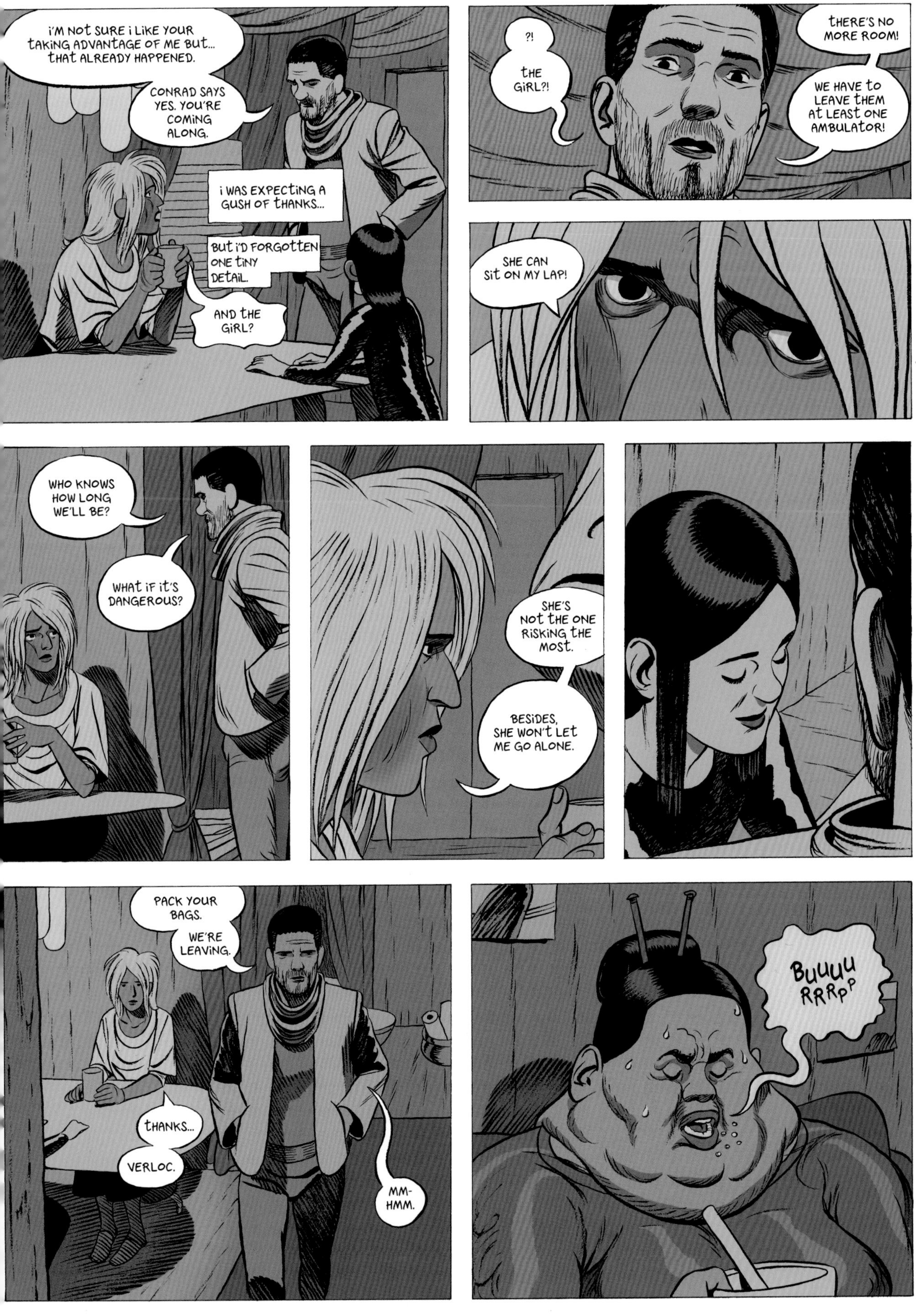
i'M NOT SURE i LIKE YOUR tAKiNG ADVANtAGE OF ME but... thAt ALREADY HAPPENED.
CONRAD SAYS YES. YOU'RE COMiNG ALONG.
i WAS EXPECtiNG A GUSH OF thANKS...
but i'D FORGOttEN ONE tiNY DEtAiL.
AND thE GiRL?
?!
thE GiRL?!
thERE'S NO MORE ROOM!
WE HAVE tO LEAVE thEM At LEASt ONE AMBULAtOR!
SHE CAN Sit ON MY LAP!
WHO KNOWS HOW LONG WE'LL BE?
WHAt iF it'S DANGEROUS?
SHE'S Not thE ONE RiSKiNG thE MOSt.
BESiDES, SHE WON'T LEt ME GO ALONE.
PACK YOUR BAGS.
WE'RE LEAViNG.
thANKS...
VERLOC.
MM-HMM.
BuuuU RRRpP

I'D PROBABLY GOTTEN CARRIED AWAY. ALL THIS UPHEAVAL IN MY LIFE HAD LEFT MY NERVES RAW AND ON EDGE. SOMETIMES WHEN I REALIZE I'M LOST ON A HOSTILE PLANET AT THE EDGE OF THE KNOWN UNIVERSE, I HAVE A BAD MOMENT.

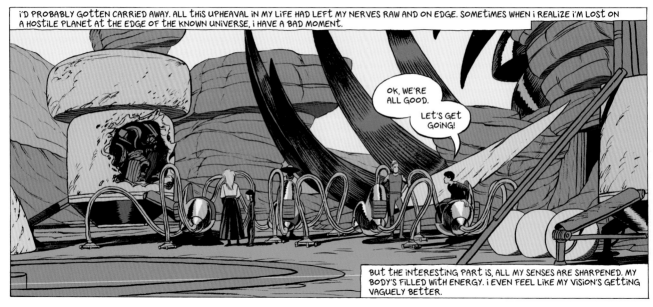

OK, WE'RE ALL GOOD.

LET'S GET GOING!

BUT THE INTERESTING PART IS, ALL MY SENSES ARE SHARPENED. MY BODY'S FILLED WITH ENERGY. I EVEN FEEL LIKE MY VISION'S GETTING VAGUELY BETTER.

THE MORNING'S BIG THRILL IS MY GETTING INTO AN AMBULATOR FOR THE FIRST TIME.

KIND OF SILLY, BUT THIS MACHINE MAKES ME GIDDY AS A LITTLE KID.

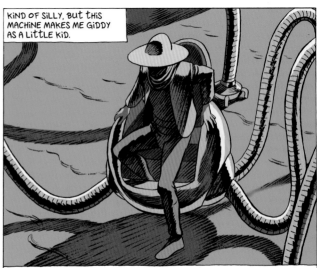

USUALLY YOU'D PILOT IT WITH BRAINWAVES, BUT SINCE EVERYONE HAD TO SWITCH OFF THEIR IMPLANTS 'CAUSE OF THE ROBOTS, CHURCHILL'S THE ONE DRIVING REMOTELY.

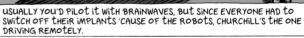

?!

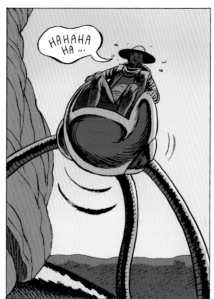

HAHAHA HA...

AWESOME!

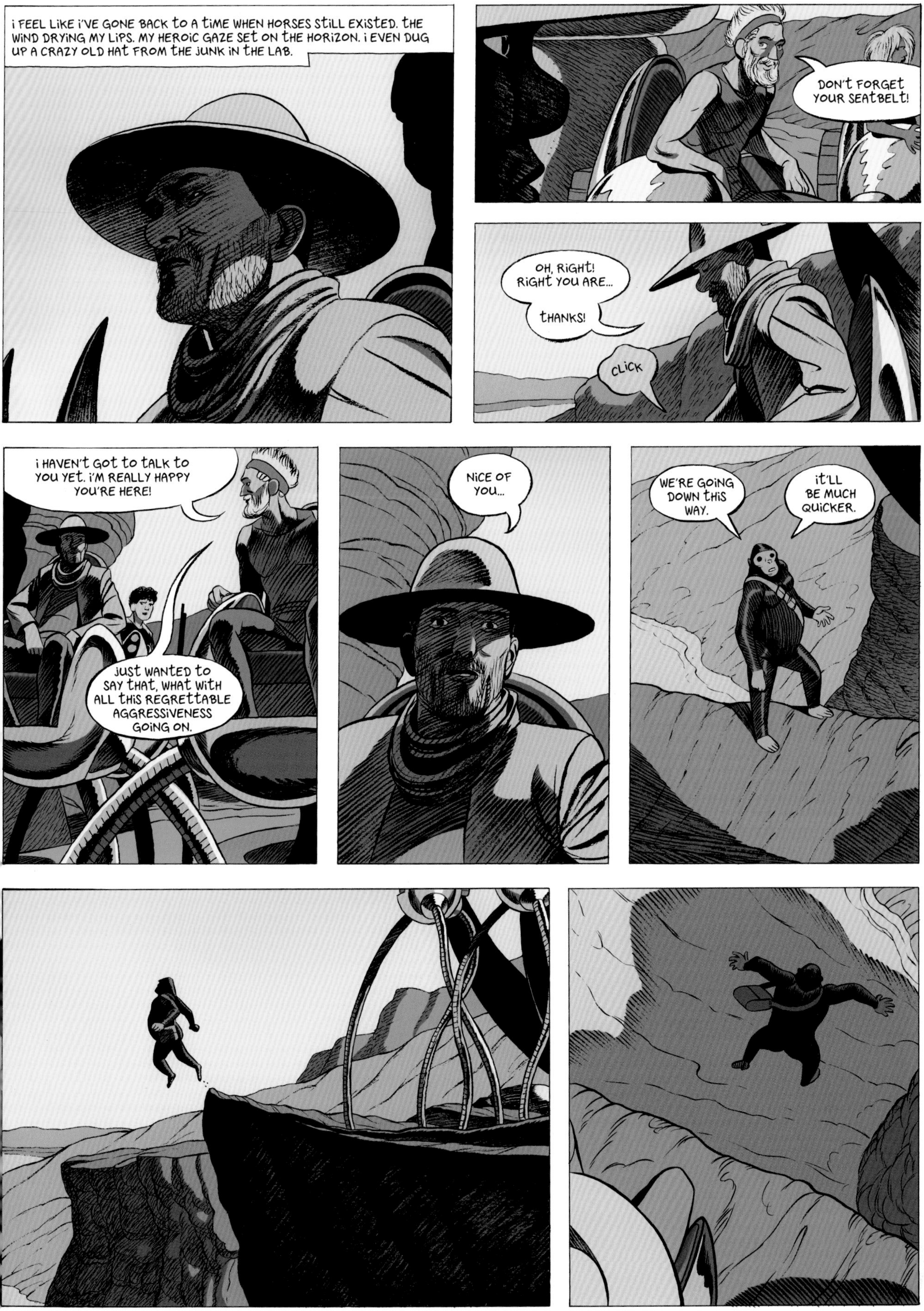

i FEEL LIKE i'VE GONE BACK to A tiME WHEN HORSES StiLL EXiStED. tHE WiND DRYiNG MY LiPS. MY HEROiC GAZE SEt ON tHE HORiZON. i EVEN DUG UP A CRAZY OLD HAt FROM tHE JUNK iN tHE LAB.
DON't FORGEt YOUR SEAtBELt!
OH, RiGHt! RiGHt YOU ARE...
tHANKS!
CLiCK
i HAVEN't Got to tALK to YOU YEt. i'M REALLY HAPPY YOU'RE HERE!
JUSt WANtED to SAY tHAt, WHAt WitH ALL tHiS REGREttABLE AGGRESSiVENESS GOiNG ON.
NiCE OF YOU...
WE'RE GOiNG DOWN tHiS WAY.
it'LL BE MUCH QUiCKER.

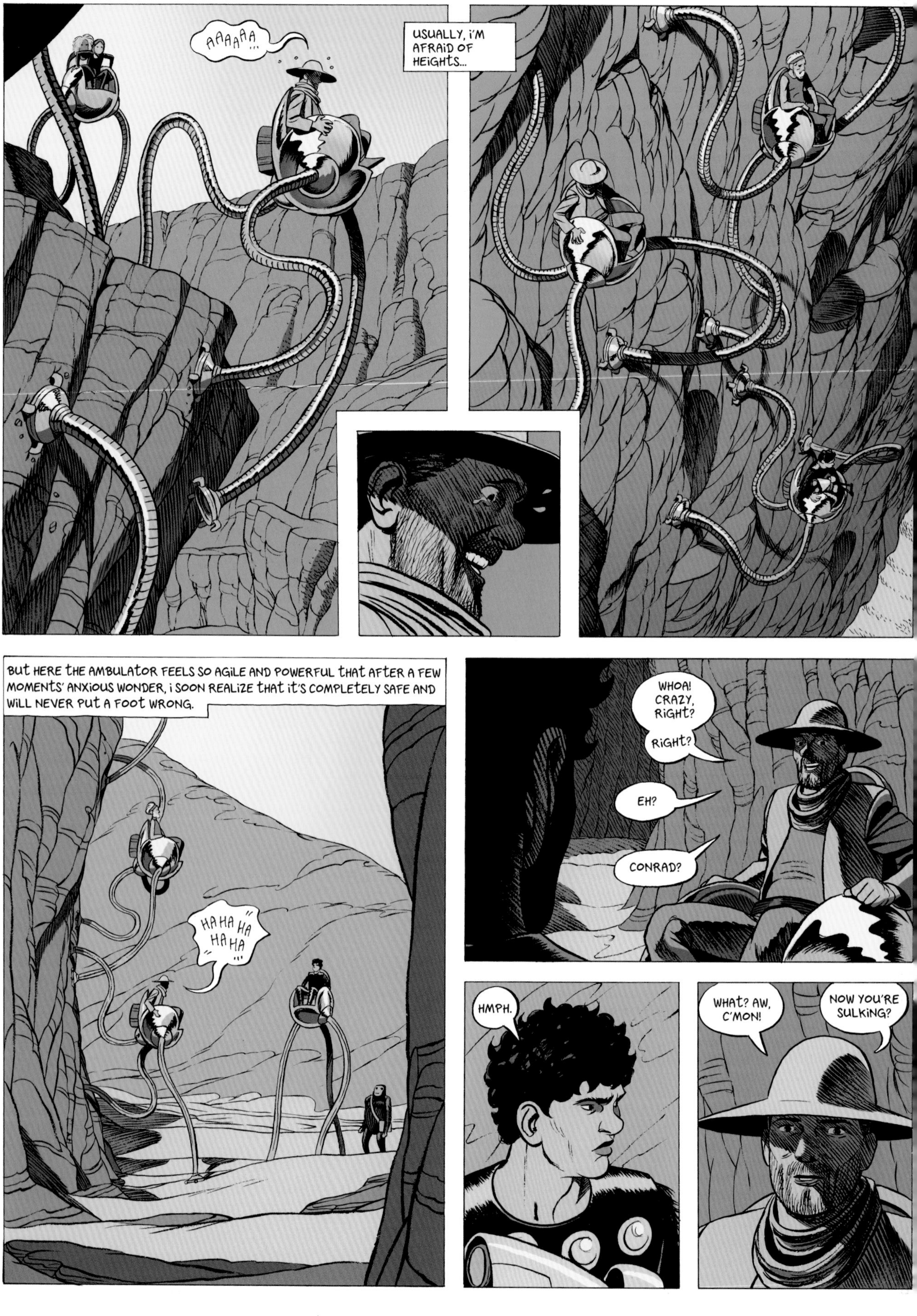
AAAAAA...
USUALLY, I'M AFRAID OF HEIGHTS...
BUT HERE THE AMBULATOR FEELS SO AGILE AND POWERFUL THAT AFTER A FEW MOMENTS' ANXIOUS WONDER, I SOON REALIZE THAT IT'S COMPLETELY SAFE AND WILL NEVER PUT A FOOT WRONG.
HA HA HA HA HA HA
WHOA! CRAZY, RIGHT?
RIGHT?
EH?
CONRAD?
HMPH.
WHAT? AW, C'MON!
NOW YOU'RE SULKING?

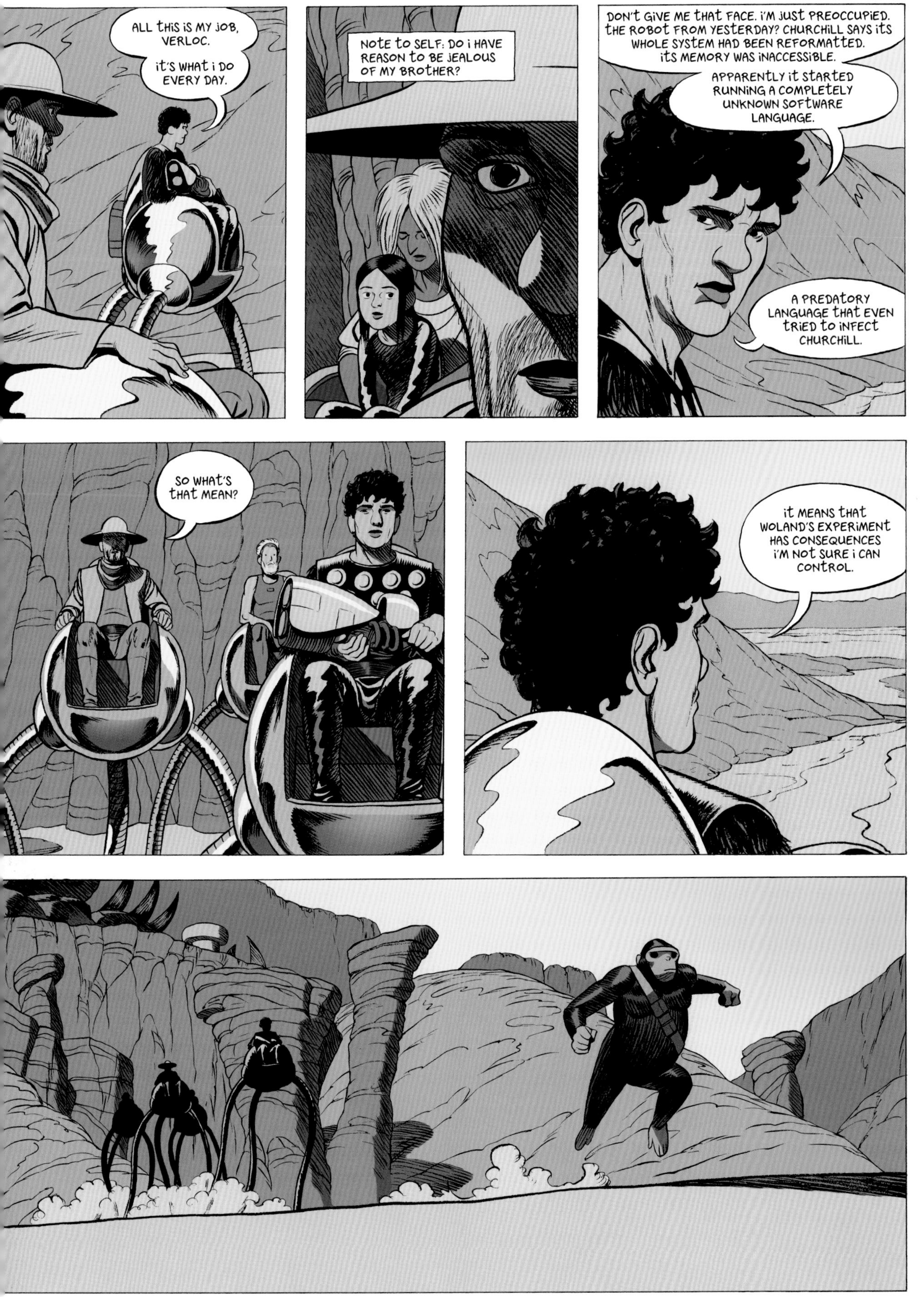

ALL THIS IS MY JOB, VERLOC.
IT'S WHAT I DO EVERY DAY.
NOTE TO SELF: DO I HAVE REASON TO BE JEALOUS OF MY BROTHER?
DON'T GIVE ME THAT FACE. I'M JUST PREOCCUPIED. THE ROBOT FROM YESTERDAY? CHURCHILL SAYS ITS WHOLE SYSTEM HAD BEEN REFORMATTED. ITS MEMORY WAS INACCESSIBLE.
APPARENTLY IT STARTED RUNNING A COMPLETELY UNKNOWN SOFTWARE LANGUAGE.
A PREDATORY LANGUAGE THAT EVEN TRIED TO INFECT CHURCHILL.
SO WHAT'S THAT MEAN?
IT MEANS THAT WOLAND'S EXPERIMENT HAS CONSEQUENCES I'M NOT SURE I CAN CONTROL.

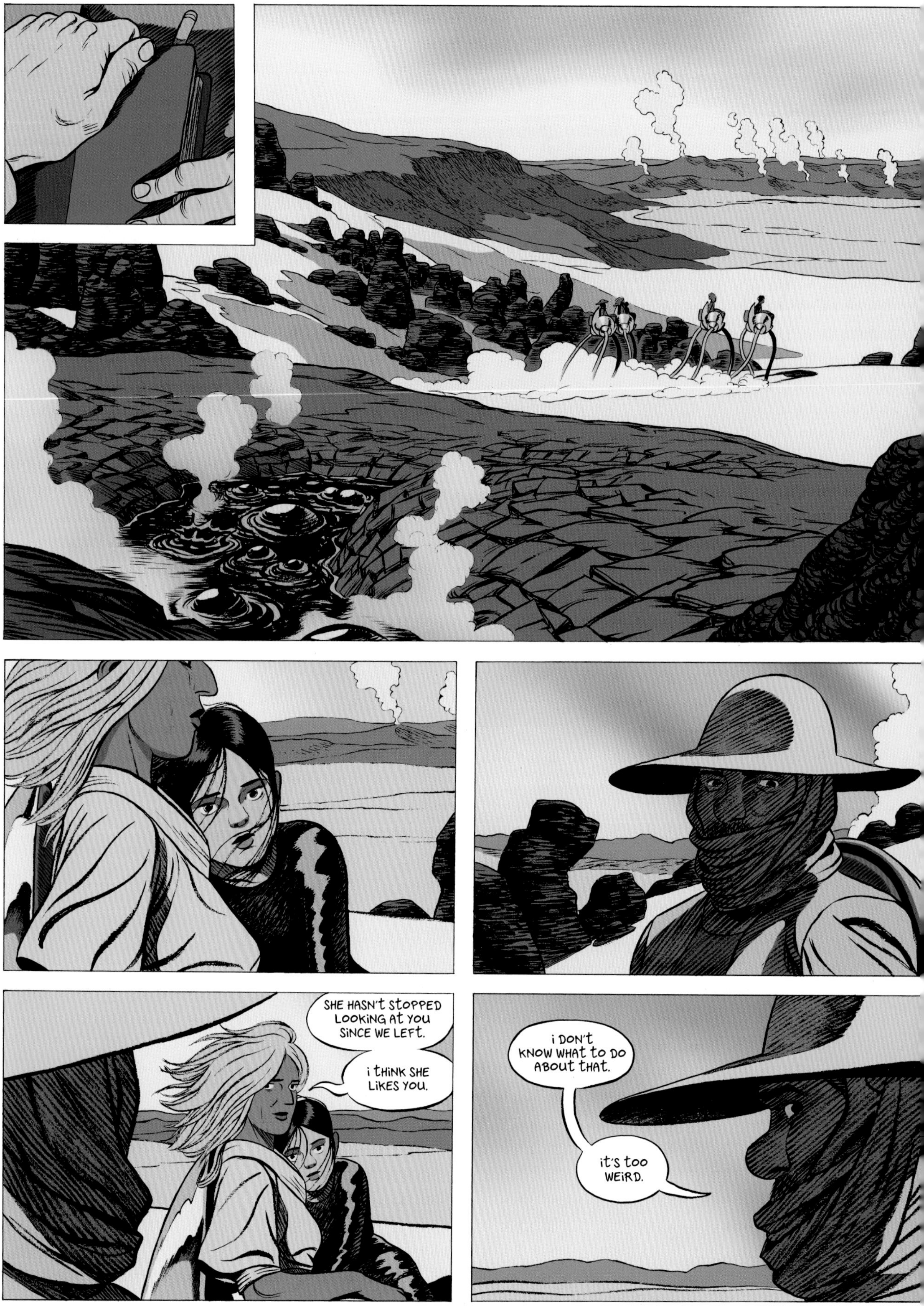
SHE HASN'T STOPPED LOOKING AT YOU SINCE WE LEFT.
i THINK SHE LIKES YOU.
i DON'T KNOW WHAT TO DO ABOUT THAT.
iT'S TOO WEiRD.

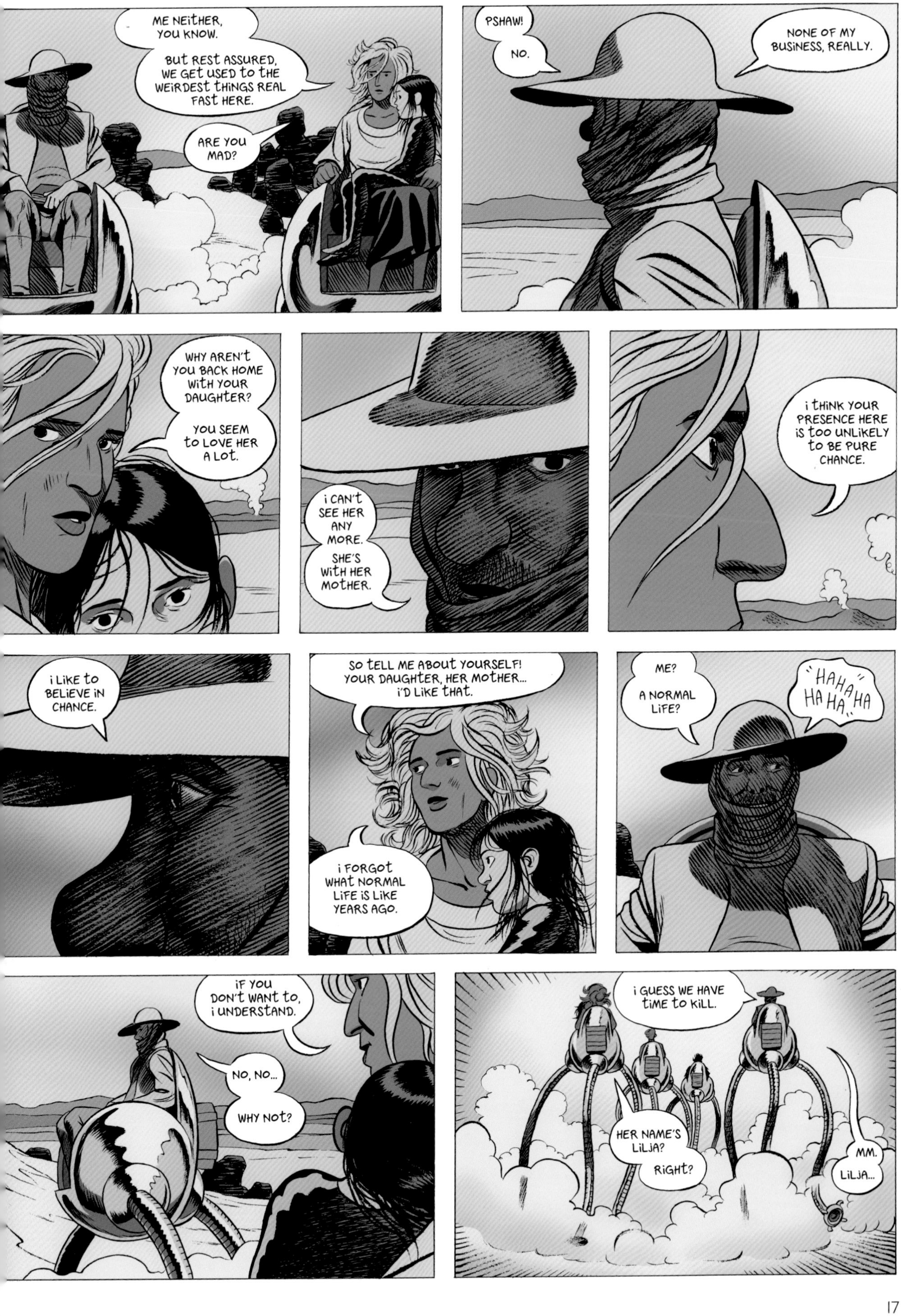
ME NEITHER, YOU KNOW.
BUT REST ASSURED, WE GET USED TO THE WEIRDEST THINGS REAL FAST HERE.
ARE YOU MAD?
PSHAW!
NO.
NONE OF MY BUSINESS, REALLY.
WHY AREN'T YOU BACK HOME WITH YOUR DAUGHTER?
YOU SEEM TO LOVE HER A LOT.
I CAN'T SEE HER ANY MORE.
SHE'S WITH HER MOTHER.
I THINK YOUR PRESENCE HERE IS TOO UNLIKELY TO BE PURE CHANCE.
I LIKE TO BELIEVE IN CHANCE.
SO TELL ME ABOUT YOURSELF! YOUR DAUGHTER, HER MOTHER... I'D LIKE THAT.
I FORGOT WHAT NORMAL LIFE IS LIKE YEARS AGO.
ME?
A NORMAL LIFE?
HAHAHA HAHAHA
IF YOU DON'T WANT TO, I UNDERSTAND.
NO, NO...
WHY NOT?
I GUESS WE HAVE TIME TO KILL.
HER NAME'S LILJA?
RIGHT?
MM.
LILJA...

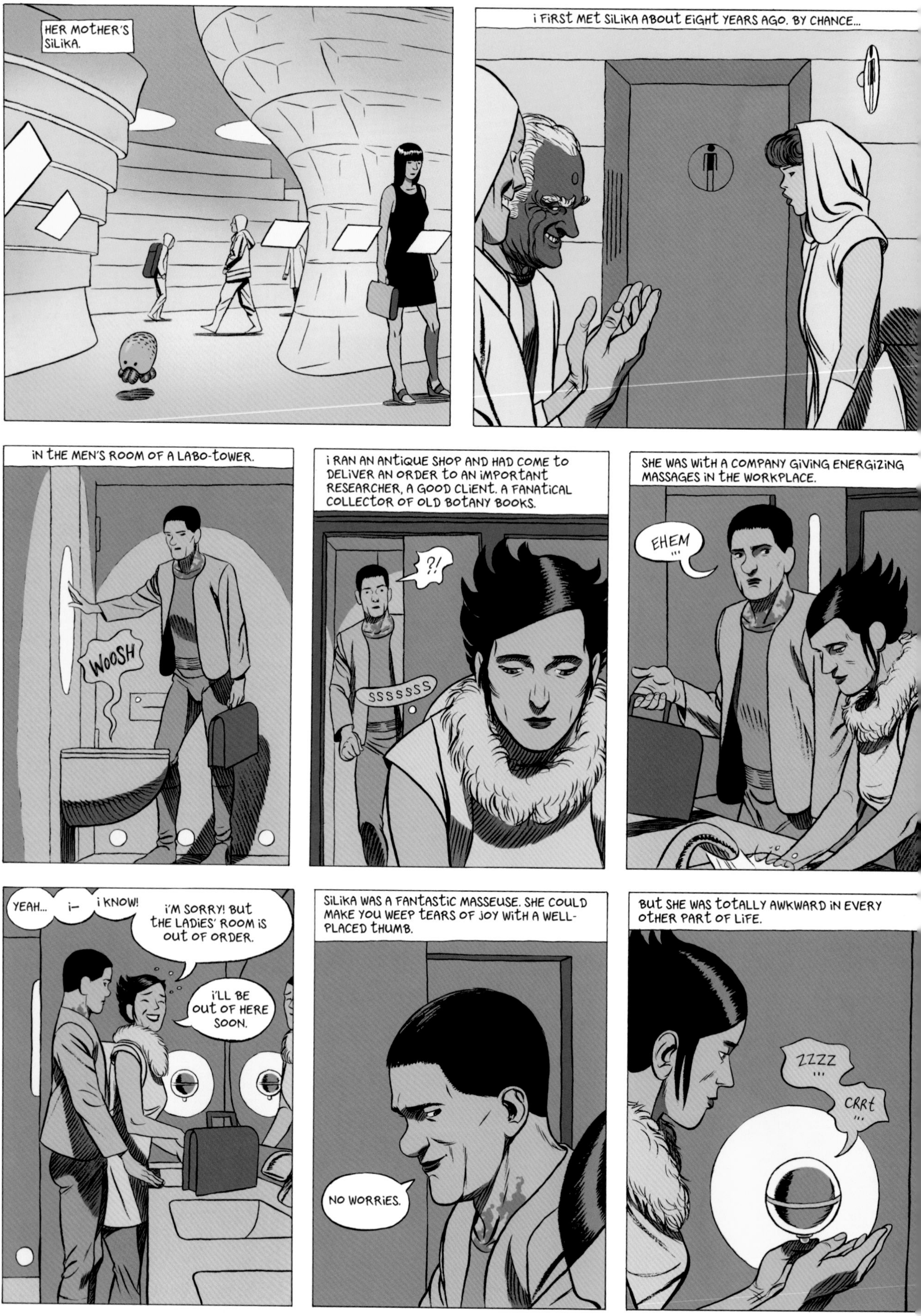
HER MOTHER'S SILIKA.
I FIRST MET SILIKA ABOUT EIGHT YEARS AGO. BY CHANCE...
IN THE MEN'S ROOM OF A LABO-TOWER.
WOOSH
I RAN AN ANTIQUE SHOP AND HAD COME TO DELIVER AN ORDER TO AN IMPORTANT RESEARCHER, A GOOD CLIENT. A FANATICAL COLLECTOR OF OLD BOTANY BOOKS.
?!
SSSSSSS
SHE WAS WITH A COMPANY GIVING ENERGIZING MASSAGES IN THE WORKPLACE.
EHEM ...
YEAH...
I–
I KNOW!
I'M SORRY! BUT THE LADIES' ROOM IS OUT OF ORDER.
I'LL BE OUT OF HERE SOON.
SILIKA WAS A FANTASTIC MASSEUSE. SHE COULD MAKE YOU WEEP TEARS OF JOY WITH A WELL-PLACED THUMB.
NO WORRIES.
BUT SHE WAS TOTALLY AWKWARD IN EVERY OTHER PART OF LIFE.
ZZZZ ...
CRRT ...

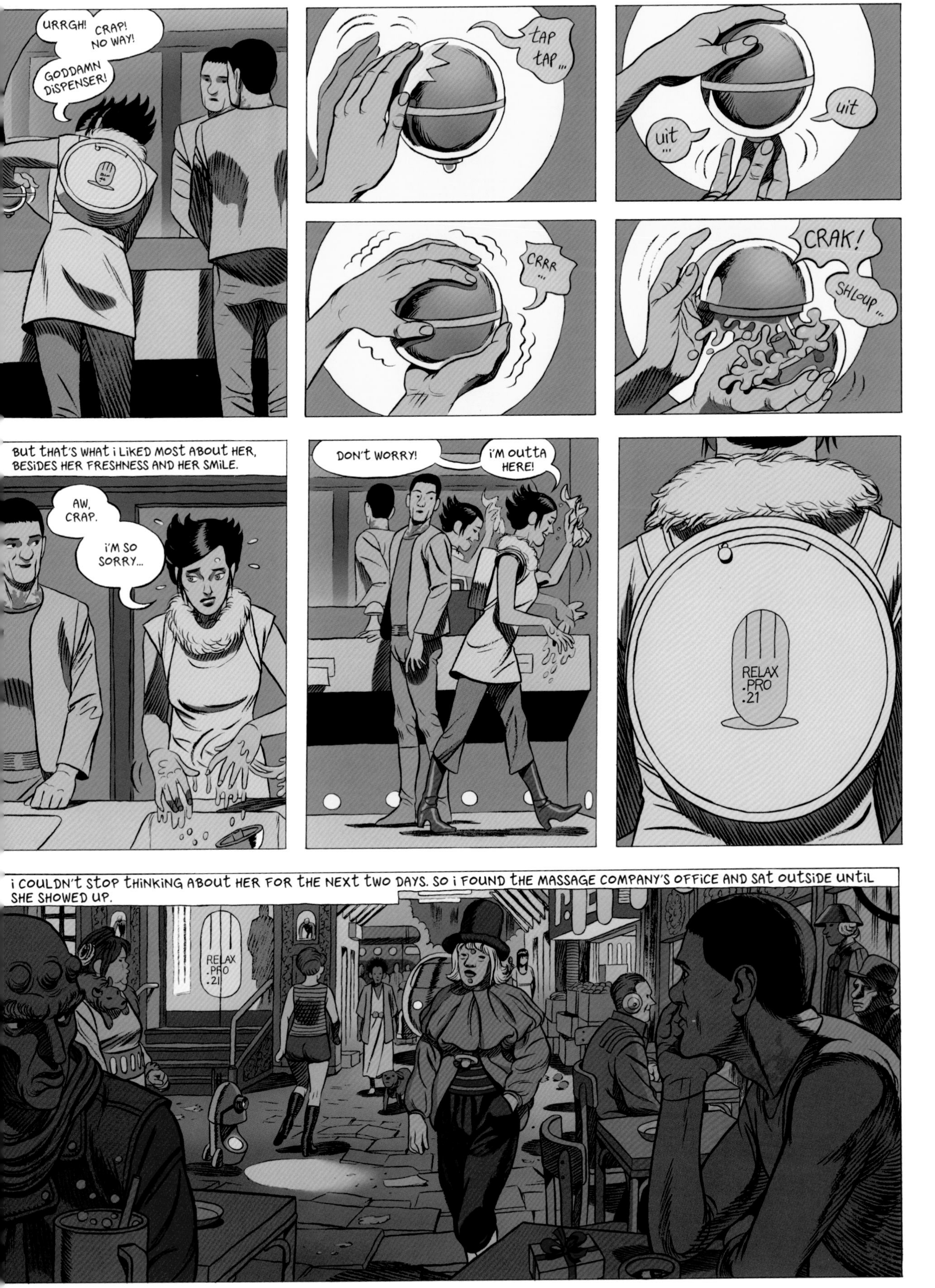

URRGH!
CRAP! NO WAY!
GODDAMN DISPENSER!
tap tap...
uit ...
uit
CRRR ...
CRAK!
SHLoup...
But that's what i liked most about her, besides her freshness and her smile.
AW, CRAP.
i'M SO SORRY...
DON'T WORRY!
i'M OUTTA HERE!
RELAX .PRO .21
i couldn't stop thinking about her for the next two days. So i found the massage company's office and sat outside until she showed up.
RELAX .PRO .21

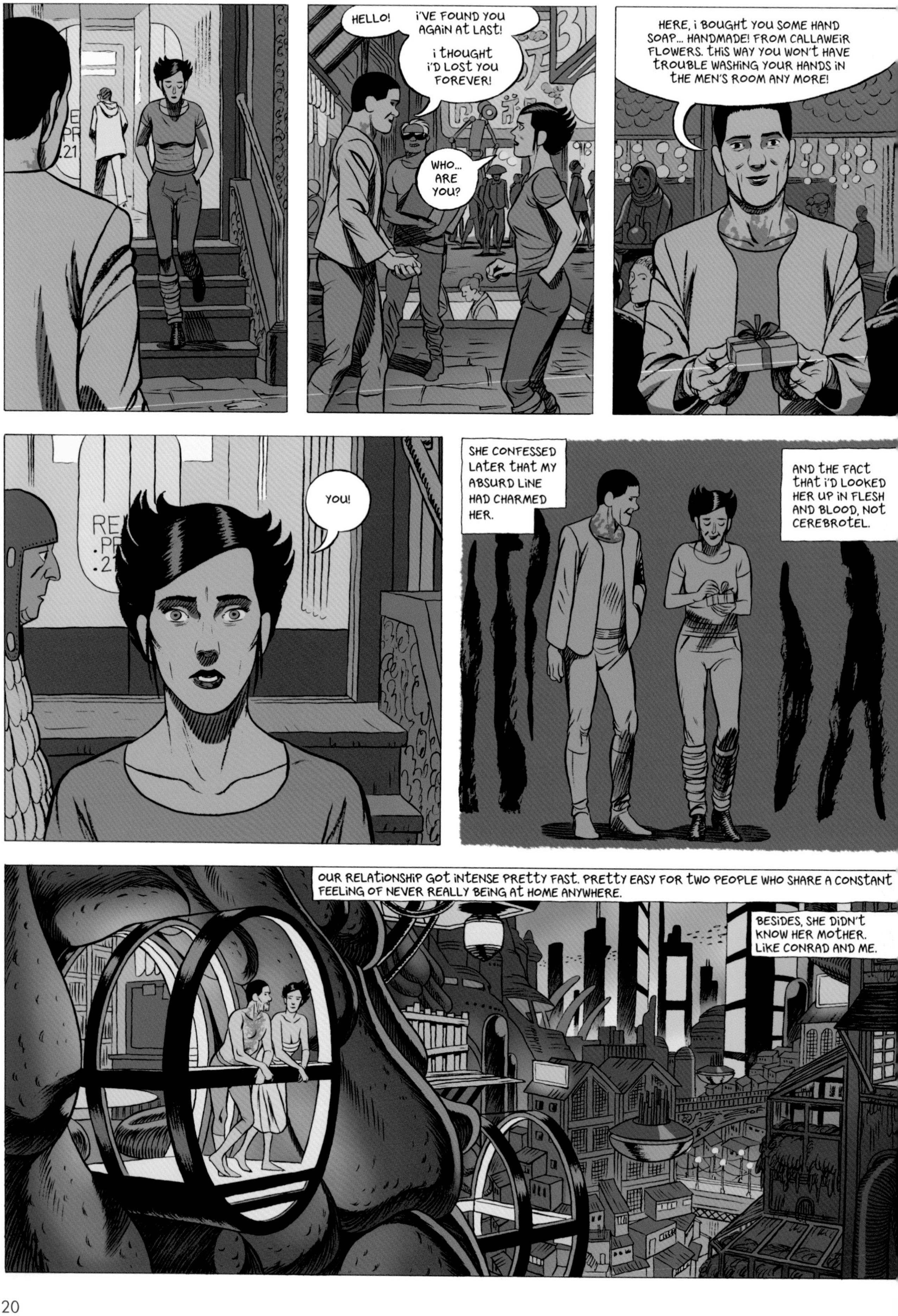
HELLO!
i'VE FOUND YOU AGAIN AT LAST!
i THOUGHT i'D LOST YOU FOREVER!
WHO... ARE YOU?
HERE, i BOUGHT YOU SOME HAND SOAP... HANDMADE! FROM CALLAWEIR FLOWERS. THIS WAY YOU WON'T HAVE TROUBLE WASHING YOUR HANDS IN THE MEN'S ROOM ANY MORE!
YOU!
SHE CONFESSED LATER THAT MY ABSURD LiNE HAD CHARMED HER.
AND THE FACT THAT i'D LOOKED HER UP iN FLESH AND BLOOD, NOT CEREBROTEL.
OUR RELATIONSHiP GOT iNTENSE PRETTY FAST. PRETTY EASY FOR TWO PEOPLE WHO SHARE A CONSTANT FEELiNG OF NEVER REALLY BEiNG AT HOME ANYWHERE.
BESiDES, SHE DiDN'T KNOW HER MOTHER. LiKE CONRAD AND ME.

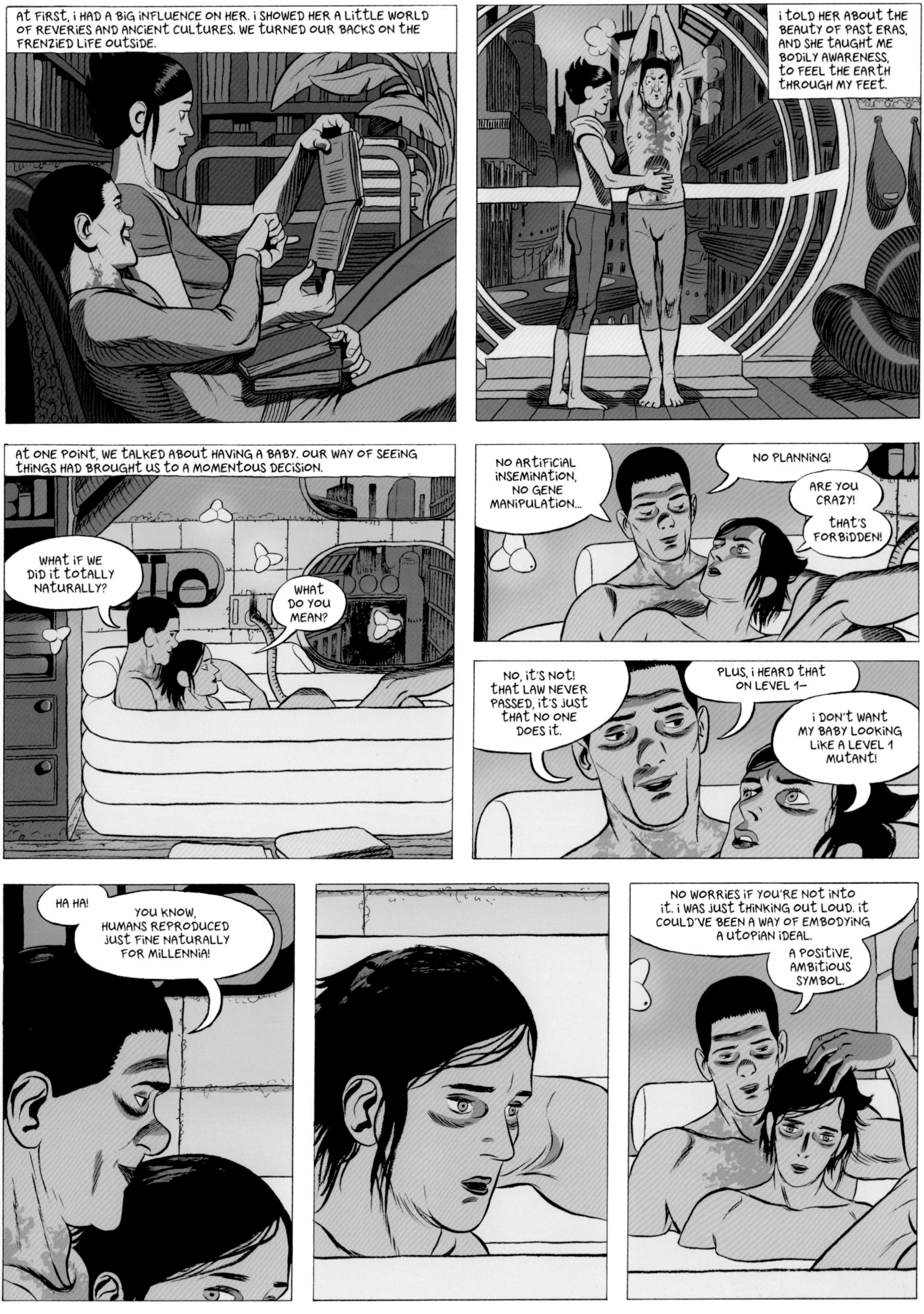

AT FIRST, I HAD A BIG INFLUENCE ON HER. I SHOWED HER A LITTLE WORLD OF REVERIES AND ANCIENT CULTURES. WE TURNED OUR BACKS ON THE FRENZIED LIFE OUTSIDE.
I TOLD HER ABOUT THE BEAUTY OF PAST ERAS, AND SHE TAUGHT ME BODILY AWARENESS, TO FEEL THE EARTH THROUGH MY FEET.
AT ONE POINT, WE TALKED ABOUT HAVING A BABY. OUR WAY OF SEEING THINGS HAD BROUGHT US TO A MOMENTOUS DECISION.
WHAT IF WE DID IT TOTALLY NATURALLY?
WHAT DO YOU MEAN?
NO ARTIFICIAL INSEMINATION, NO GENE MANIPULATION...
NO PLANNING!
ARE YOU CRAZY!
THAT'S FORBIDDEN!
NO, IT'S NOT! THAT LAW NEVER PASSED, IT'S JUST THAT NO ONE DOES IT.
PLUS, I HEARD THAT ON LEVEL 1–
I DON'T WANT MY BABY LOOKING LIKE A LEVEL 1 MUTANT!
HA HA!
YOU KNOW, HUMANS REPRODUCED JUST FINE NATURALLY FOR MILLENNIA!
NO WORRIES IF YOU'RE NOT INTO IT. I WAS JUST THINKING OUT LOUD. IT COULD'VE BEEN A WAY OF EMBODYING A UTOPIAN IDEAL.
A POSITIVE, AMBITIOUS SYMBOL.

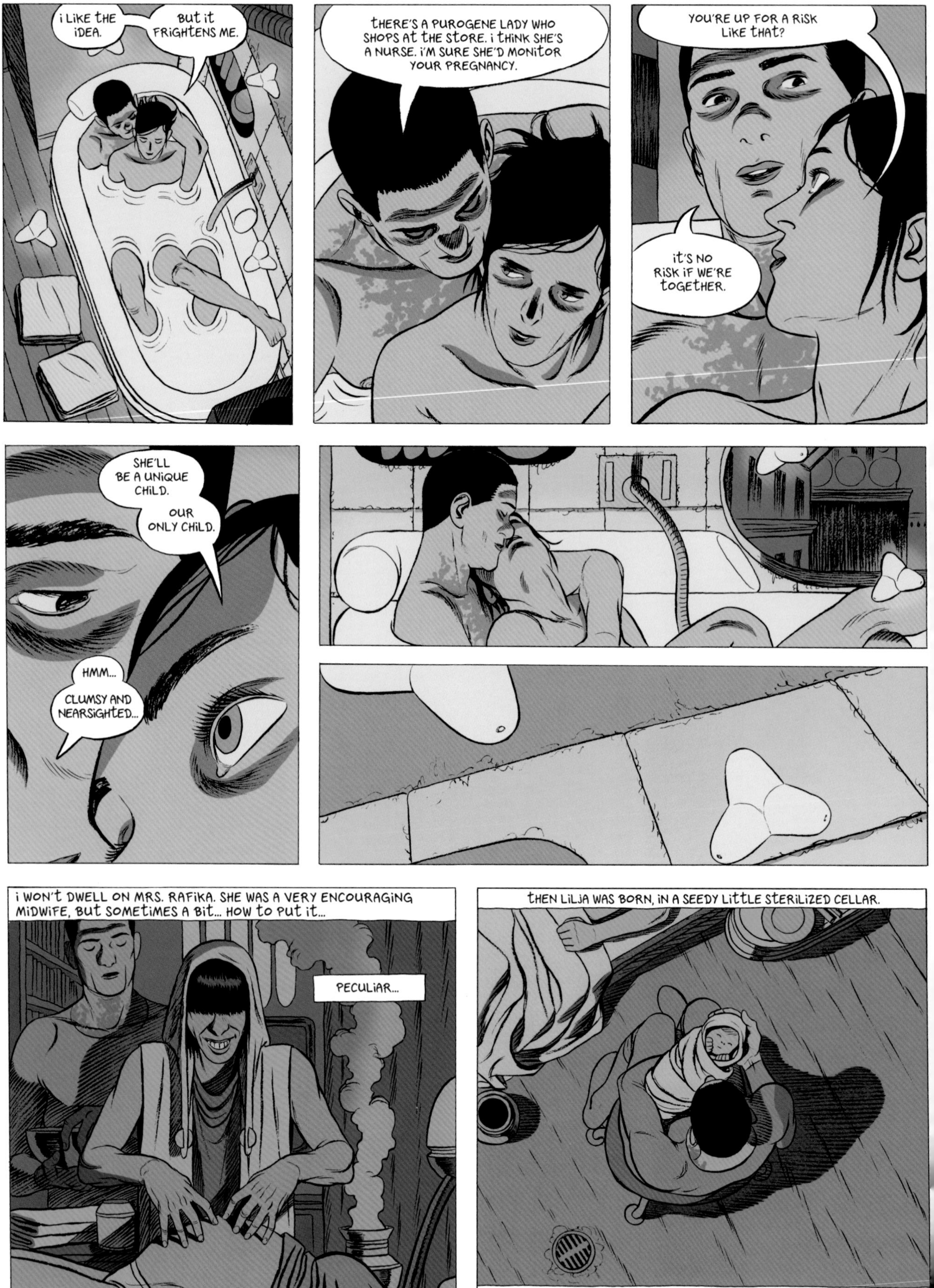
I LIKE THE IDEA.
BUT IT FRIGHTENS ME.
THERE'S A PUROGENE LADY WHO SHOPS AT THE STORE. I THINK SHE'S A NURSE. I'M SURE SHE'D MONITOR YOUR PREGNANCY.
YOU'RE UP FOR A RISK LIKE THAT?
IT'S NO RISK IF WE'RE TOGETHER.
SHE'LL BE A UNIQUE CHILD.
OUR ONLY CHILD.
HMM...
CLUMSY AND NEARSIGHTED...
I WON'T DWELL ON MRS. RAFIKA. SHE WAS A VERY ENCOURAGING MIDWIFE, BUT SOMETIMES A BIT... HOW TO PUT IT...
PECULIAR...
THEN LILJA WAS BORN, IN A SEEDY LITTLE STERILIZED CELLAR.
A WONDERFUL PROMISE OF PURITY TRAPPED BETWEEN CONCRETE WALLS.

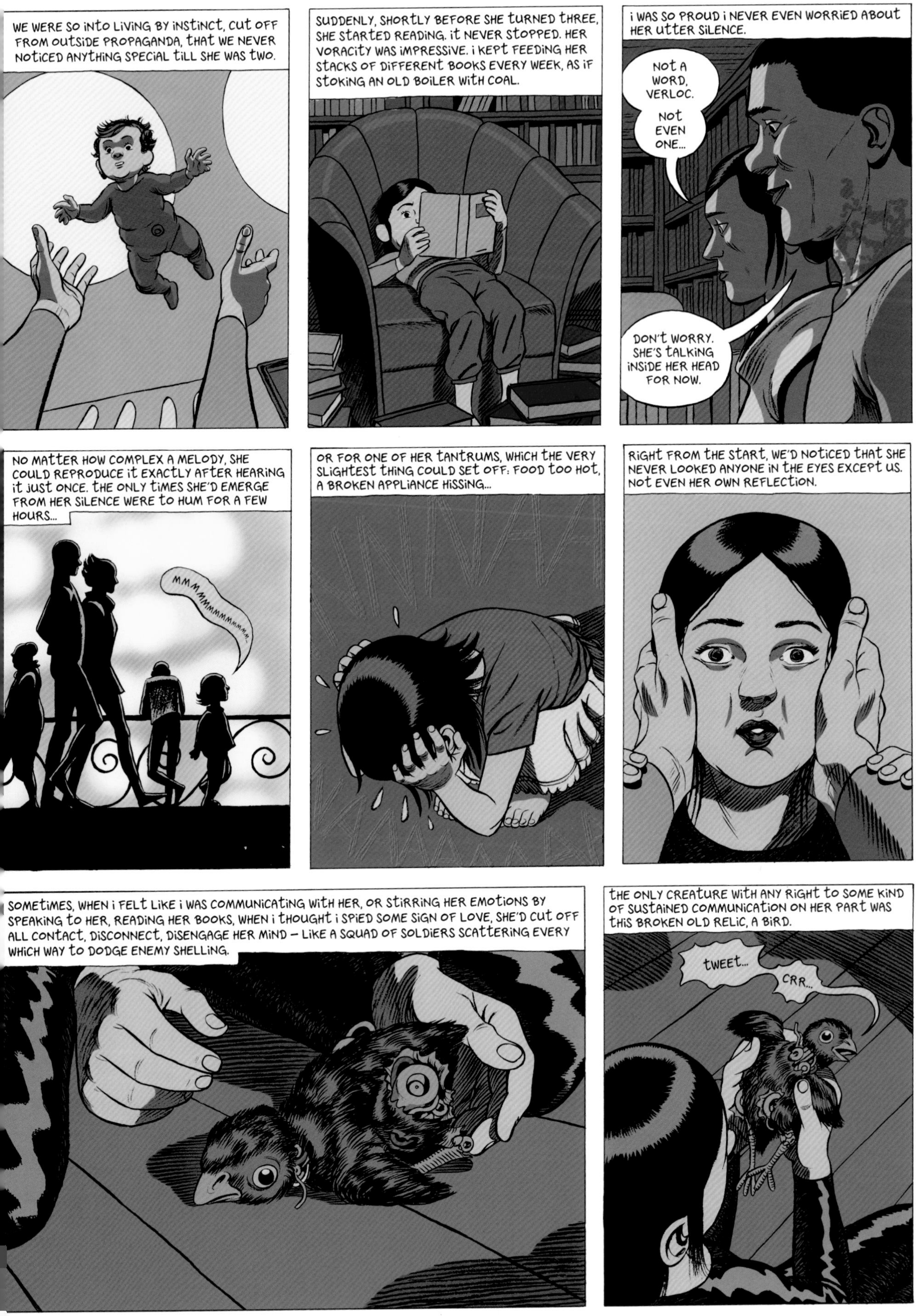
WE WERE SO INTO LIVING BY INSTINCT, CUT OFF FROM OUTSIDE PROPAGANDA, THAT WE NEVER NOTICED ANYTHING SPECIAL TILL SHE WAS TWO.
SUDDENLY, SHORTLY BEFORE SHE TURNED THREE, SHE STARTED READING. IT NEVER STOPPED. HER VORACITY WAS IMPRESSIVE. I KEPT FEEDING HER STACKS OF DIFFERENT BOOKS EVERY WEEK, AS IF STOKING AN OLD BOILER WITH COAL.
I WAS SO PROUD I NEVER EVEN WORRIED ABOUT HER UTTER SILENCE.
NOT A WORD, VERLOC.
NOT EVEN ONE...
DON'T WORRY. SHE'S TALKING INSIDE HER HEAD FOR NOW.
NO MATTER HOW COMPLEX A MELODY, SHE COULD REPRODUCE IT EXACTLY AFTER HEARING IT JUST ONCE. THE ONLY TIMES SHE'D EMERGE FROM HER SILENCE WERE TO HUM FOR A FEW HOURS...
MMMMMMMMMMMMMM...
OR FOR ONE OF HER TANTRUMS, WHICH THE VERY SLIGHTEST THING COULD SET OFF: FOOD TOO HOT, A BROKEN APPLIANCE HISSING...
RIGHT FROM THE START, WE'D NOTICED THAT SHE NEVER LOOKED ANYONE IN THE EYES EXCEPT US. NOT EVEN HER OWN REFLECTION.
SOMETIMES, WHEN I FELT LIKE I WAS COMMUNICATING WITH HER, OR STIRRING HER EMOTIONS BY SPEAKING TO HER, READING HER BOOKS, WHEN I THOUGHT I SPIED SOME SIGN OF LOVE, SHE'D CUT OFF ALL CONTACT, DISCONNECT, DISENGAGE HER MIND – LIKE A SQUAD OF SOLDIERS SCATTERING EVERY WHICH WAY TO DODGE ENEMY SHELLING.
THE ONLY CREATURE WITH ANY RIGHT TO SOME KIND OF SUSTAINED COMMUNICATION ON HER PART WAS THIS BROKEN OLD RELIC, A BIRD.
TWEET...
CRR...

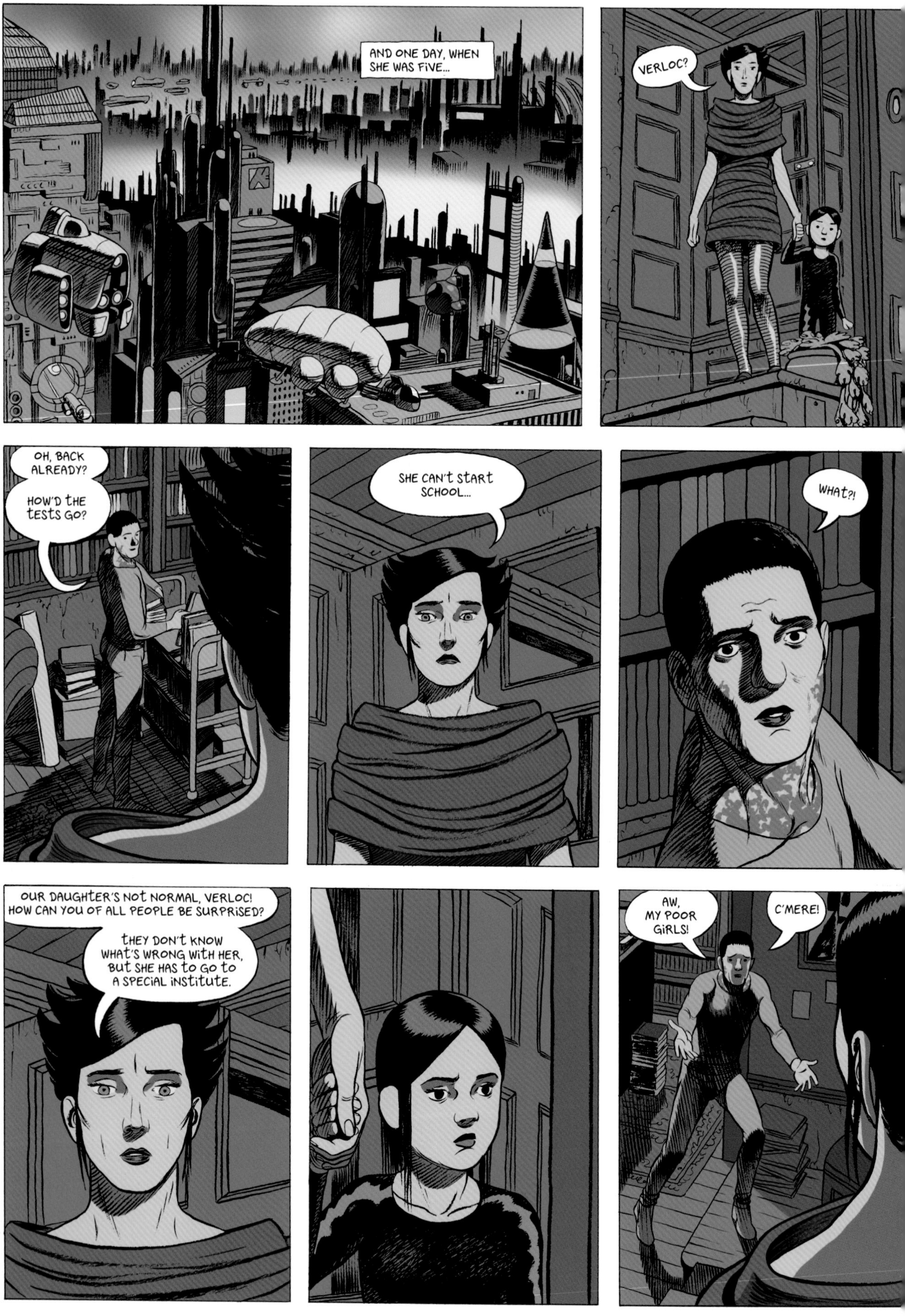
AND ONE DAY, WHEN SHE WAS FIVE...
VERLOC?
OH, BACK ALREADY?
HOW'D THE TESTS GO?
SHE CAN'T START SCHOOL...
WHAT?!
OUR DAUGHTER'S NOT NORMAL, VERLOC! HOW CAN YOU OF ALL PEOPLE BE SURPRISED?
THEY DON'T KNOW WHAT'S WRONG WITH HER, BUT SHE HAS TO GO TO A SPECIAL INSTITUTE.
AW, MY POOR GIRLS!
C'MERE!

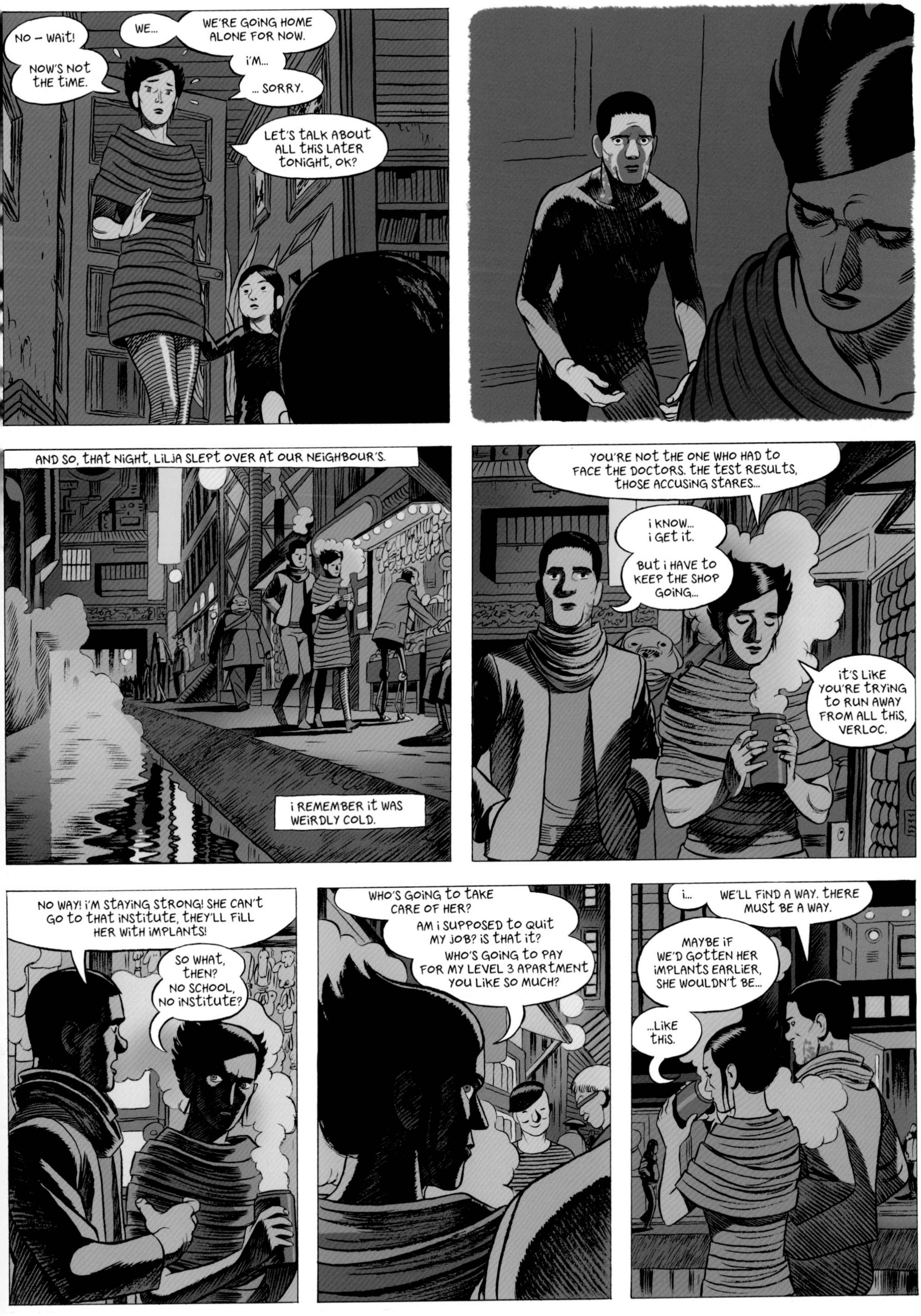
NO – WAit!
NOW'S NOt the time.
WE...
WE'RE GOiNG HOME ALONE FOR NOW.
i'M...
... SORRY.
LET'S tALK ABOUt ALL tHiS LAtER tONiGHt, OK?
AND SO, tHAt NiGHt, LiLJA SLEPt OVER At OUR NEiGHBOUR'S.
i REMEMBER it WAS WEiRDLY COLD.
YOU'RE NOt tHE ONE WHO HAD tO FACE tHE DOCtORS. tHE tESt RESULtS, tHOSE ACCUSiNG StARES...
i KNOW... i GEt it.
BUt i HAVE tO KEEP tHE SHOP GOiNG...
it'S LiKE YOU'RE tRYiNG tO RUN AWAY FROM ALL tHiS, VERLOC.
NO WAY! i'M StAYiNG StRONG! SHE CAN'T GO tO tHAt iNStitUtE, tHEY'LL FiLL HER WitH iMPLANtS!
SO WHAt, tHEN? NO SCHOOL, NO iNStitUtE?
WHO'S GOiNG tO tAKE CARE OF HER?
AM i SUPPOSED tO QUit MY JOB? iS tHAt it?
WHO'S GOiNG tO PAY FOR MY LEVEL 3 APARtMENt YOU LiKE SO MUCH?
i...
WE'LL FiND A WAY. tHERE MUSt BE A WAY.
MAYBE iF WE'D GOttEN HER iMPLANtS EARLiER, SHE WOULDN'T BE...
...LiKE tHiS.

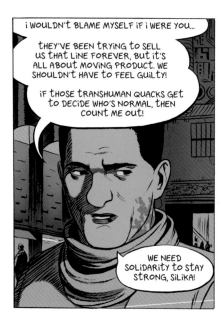

I WOULDN'T BLAME MYSELF IF I WERE YOU...

THEY'VE BEEN TRYING TO SELL US THAT LINE FOREVER, BUT IT'S ALL ABOUT MOVING PRODUCT. WE SHOULDN'T HAVE TO FEEL GUILTY!

IF THOSE TRANSHUMAN QUACKS GET TO DECIDE WHO'S NORMAL, THEN COUNT ME OUT!

WE NEED SOLIDARITY TO STAY STRONG, SILIKA!

STAY STRONG FOR WHAT?

IT'S EASY FOR YOU. YOU LIVE AMONG YOUR ANCIENT RELICS...

BUT I HAVE TO GO OUT AMONG PEOPLE FOR MY JOB. I FEEL LIKE I'M TAKING ALL THE HITS.

SILIKA NEVER LOOKED AT ME THE SAME WAY AGAIN.

HAD SHE ALREADY MET THAT OTHER GUY?

SHE'D ALWAYS ACCEPTED ME JUST AS I WAS.

TILL THEN, HER LOOK HAD BEEN ONE OF TENDERNESS, EAGERNESS, WITH A HINT OF CURIOSITY.

FROM THEN ON, SHE LOOKED LIKE A WOMAN TRYING HARD TO LOVE A MAN COVERED WITH STAINS.

GULP...

THERE MUST BE SOME ALTERNATIVE TREATMENT...

I'LL LOOK INTO IT.

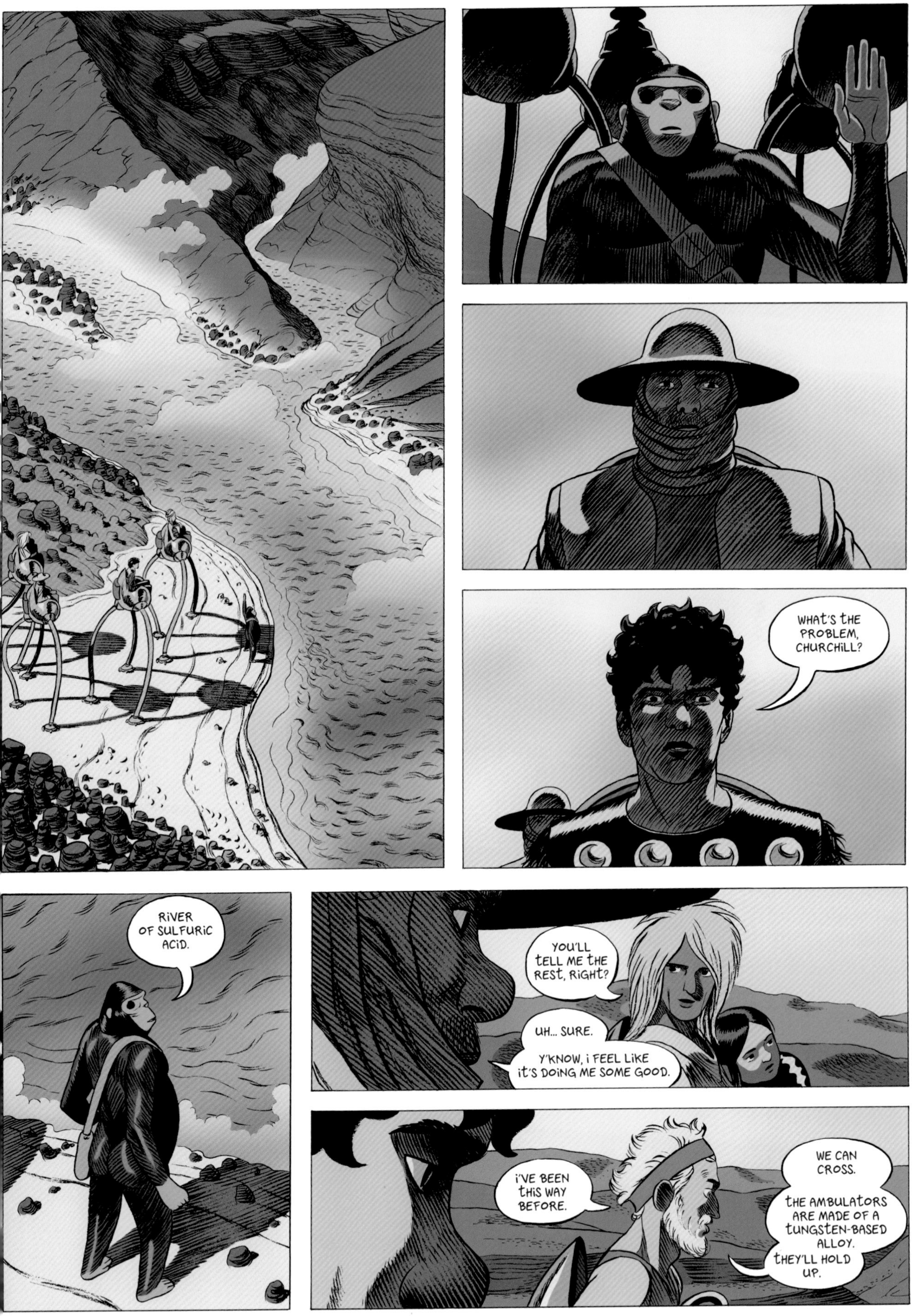
WHAT'S THE PROBLEM, CHURCHILL?
RIVER OF SULFURIC ACID.
YOU'LL TELL ME THE REST, RIGHT?
UH... SURE.
Y'KNOW, I FEEL LIKE IT'S DOING ME SOME GOOD.
I'VE BEEN THIS WAY BEFORE.
WE CAN CROSS.
THE AMBULATORS ARE MADE OF A TUNGSTEN-BASED ALLOY.
THEY'LL HOLD UP.

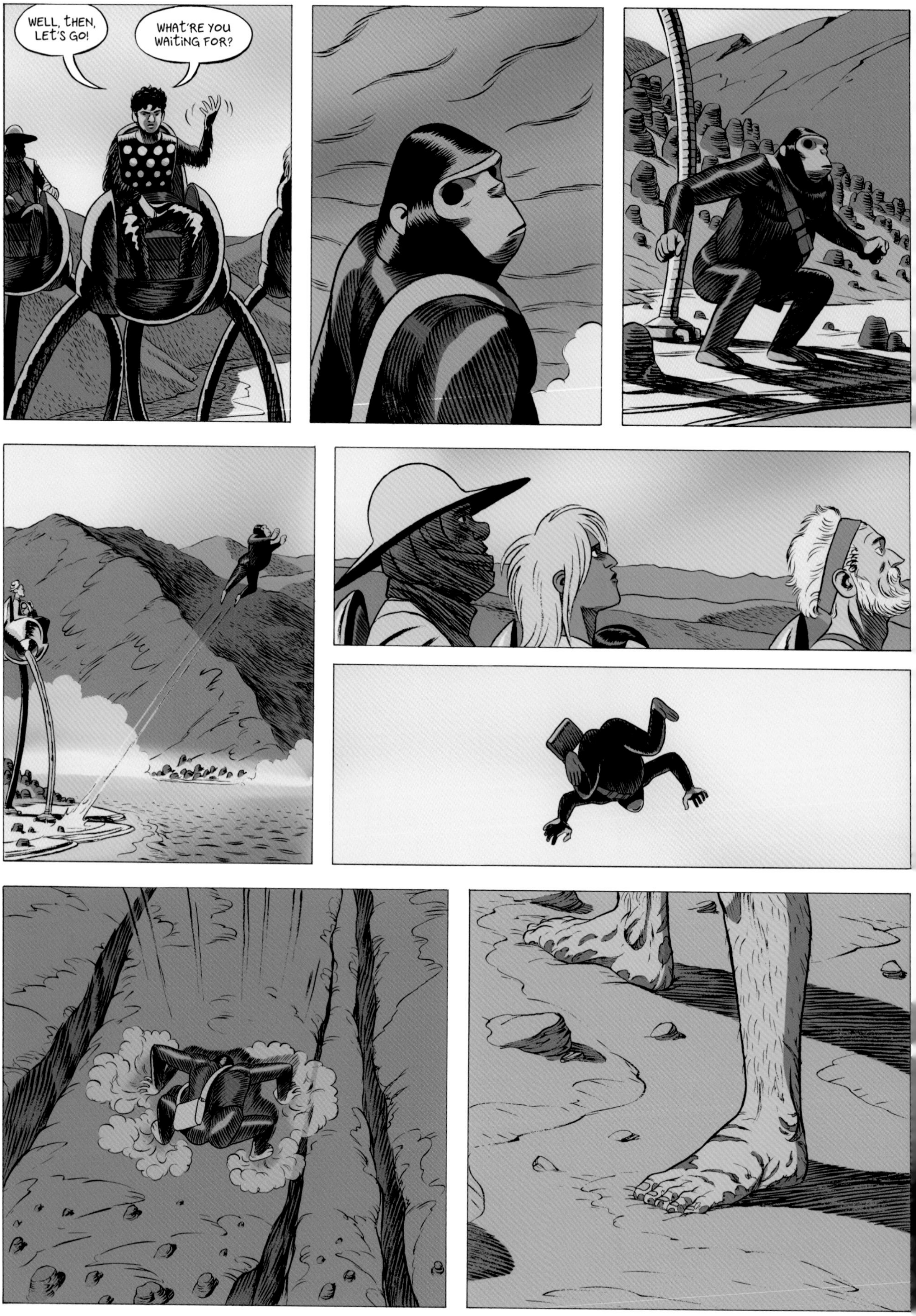
WELL, THEN, LET'S GO!
WHAT'RE YOU WAITING FOR?

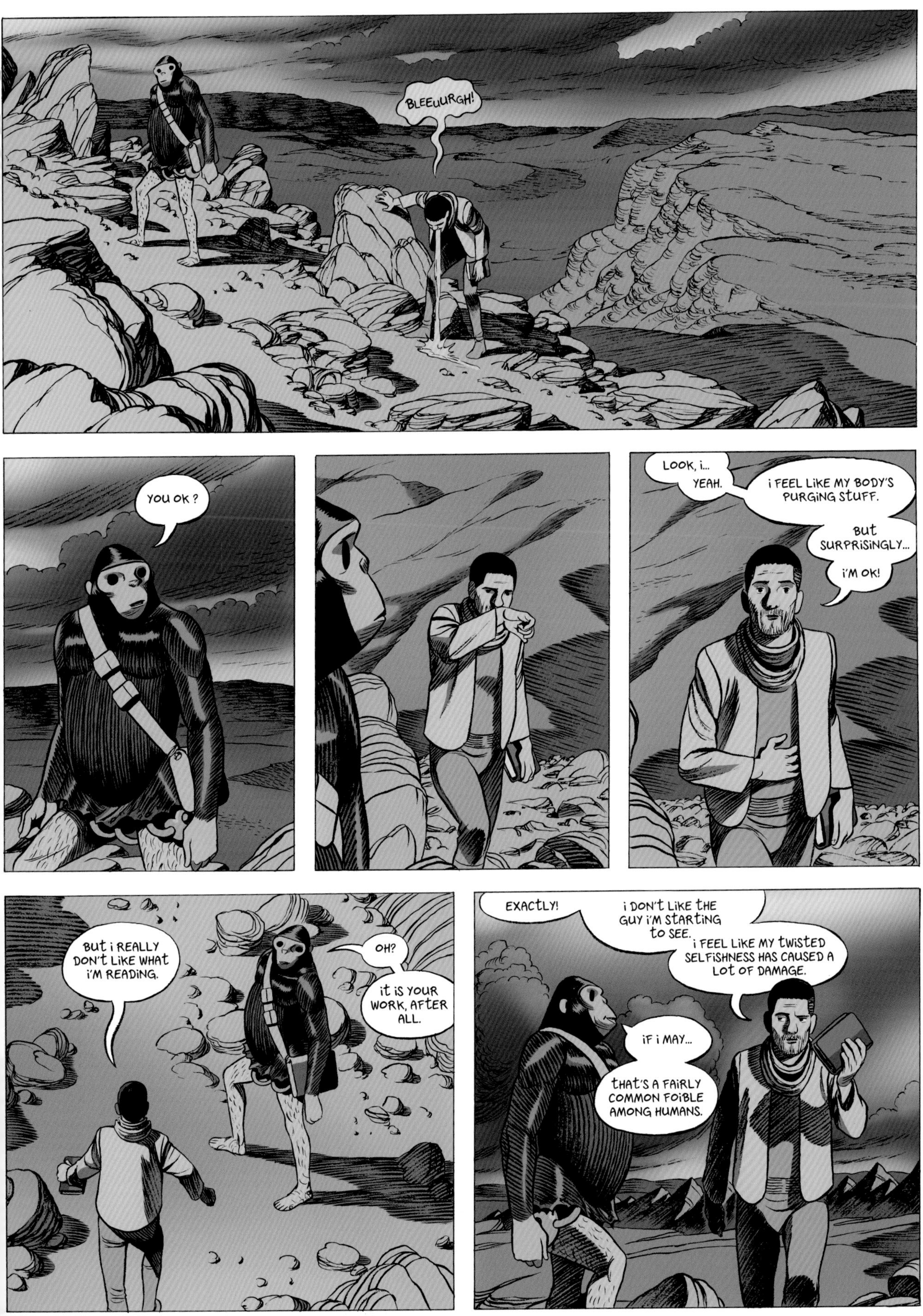
BLEEUURGH!
YOU OK ?
LOOK, i...
YEAH.
i FEEL LiKE MY BODY'S PURGiNG STUFF.
BUT SURPRiSiNGLY...
i'M OK!
BUT i REALLY DON'T LiKE WHAT i'M READiNG.
OH?
iT iS YOUR WORK, AFTER ALL.
EXACTLY!
i DON'T LiKE THE GUY i'M STARTiNG TO SEE.
i FEEL LiKE MY TWiSTED SELFiSHNESS HAS CAUSED A LOT OF DAMAGE.
iF i MAY...
THAT'S A FAiRLY COMMON FOiBLE AMONG HUMANS.

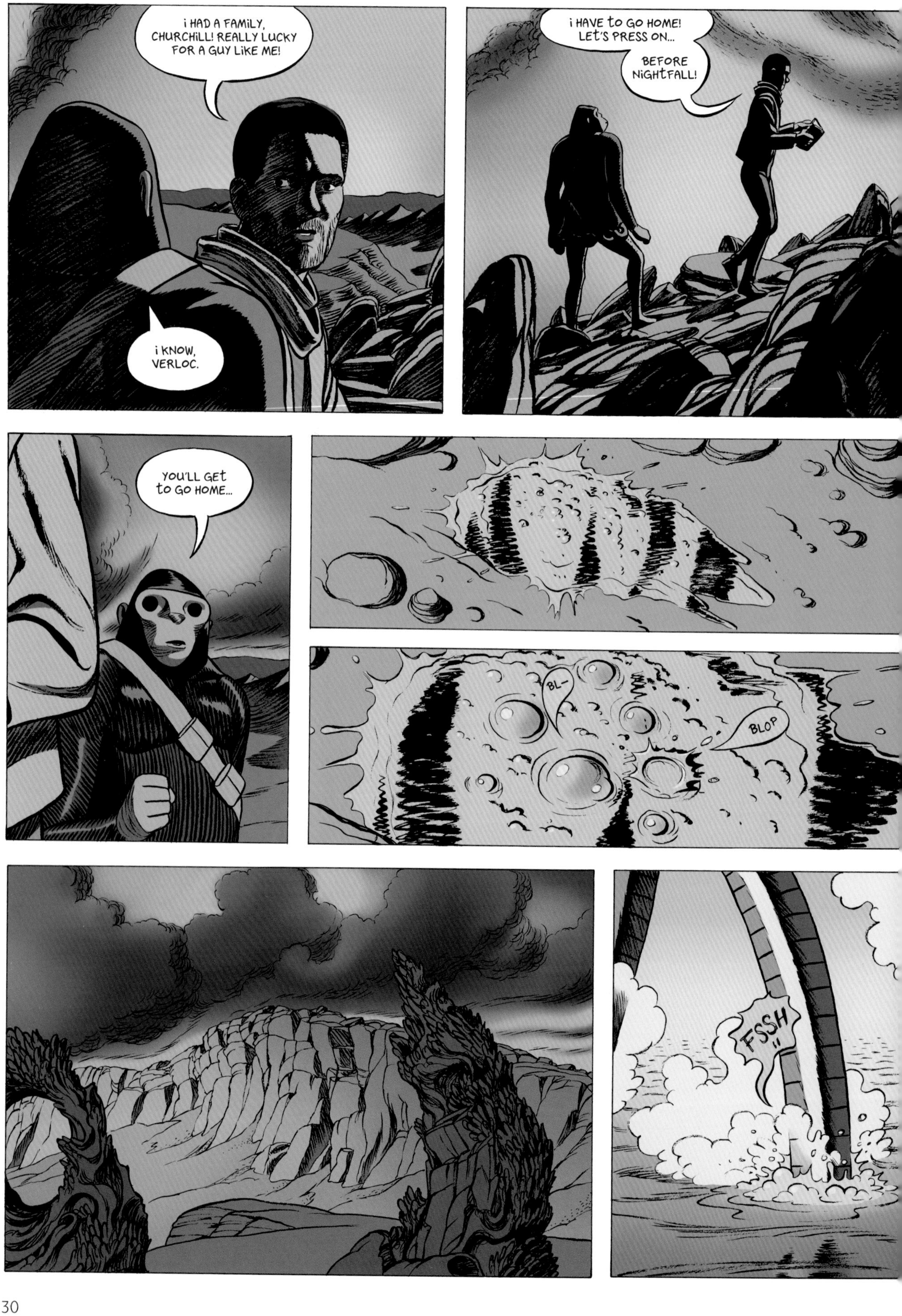

i HAD A FAMiLY, CHURCHiLL! REALLY LUCKY FOR A GUY LiKE ME!
i KNOW, VERLOC.
i HAVE to GO HOME! LET'S PRESS ON...
BEFORE NiGHtFALL!
YOU'LL GEt to GO HOME...
BL-
BLOP
FSSH!!

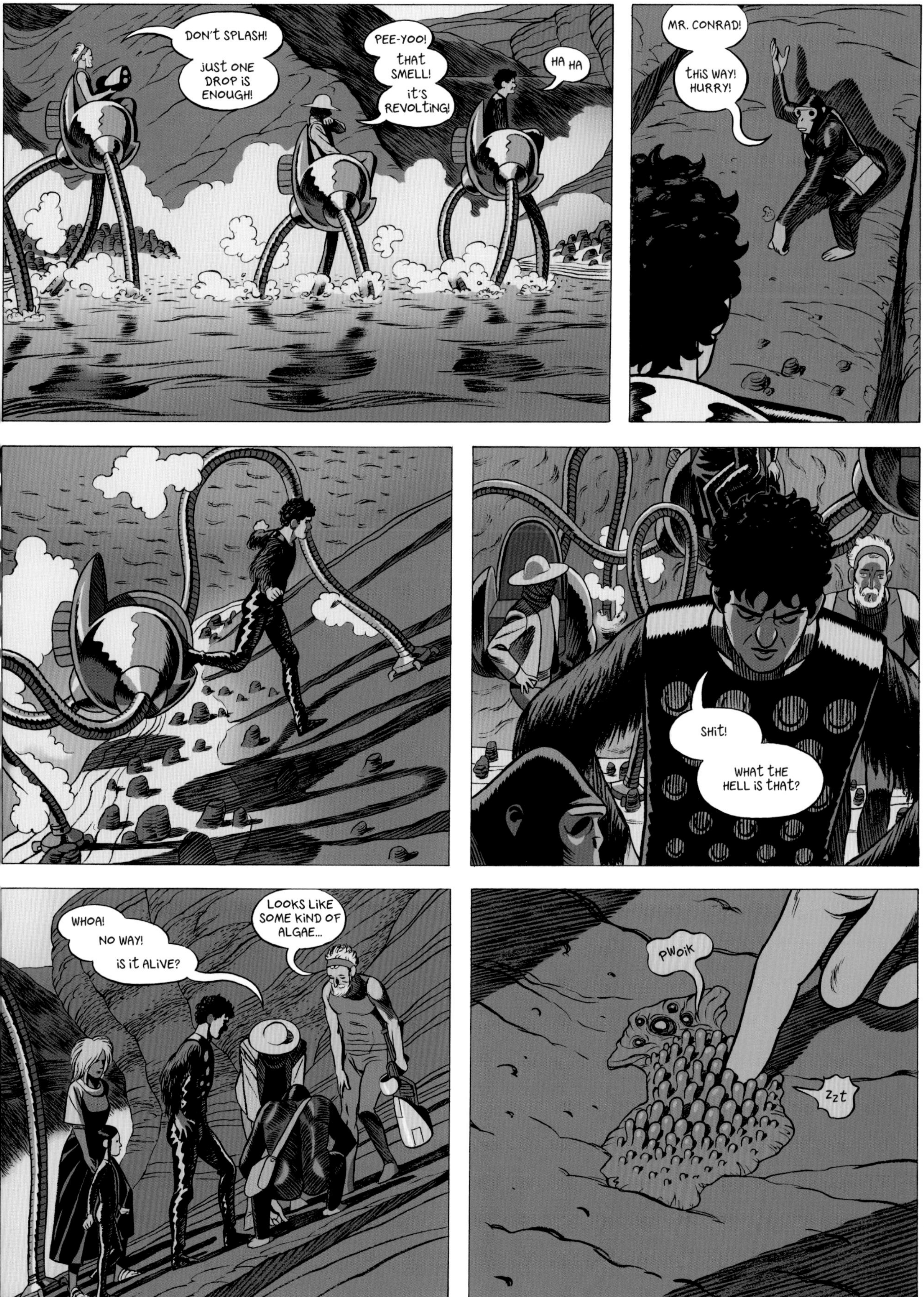
DON'T SPLASH!
JUST ONE DROP IS ENOUGH!
PEE-YOO!
THAT SMELL!
IT'S REVOLTING!
HA HA
MR. CONRAD!
THIS WAY! HURRY!
SHIT!
WHAT THE HELL IS THAT?
WHOA!
NO WAY!
IS IT ALIVE?
LOOKS LIKE SOME KIND OF ALGAE...
PWOIK
ZZT

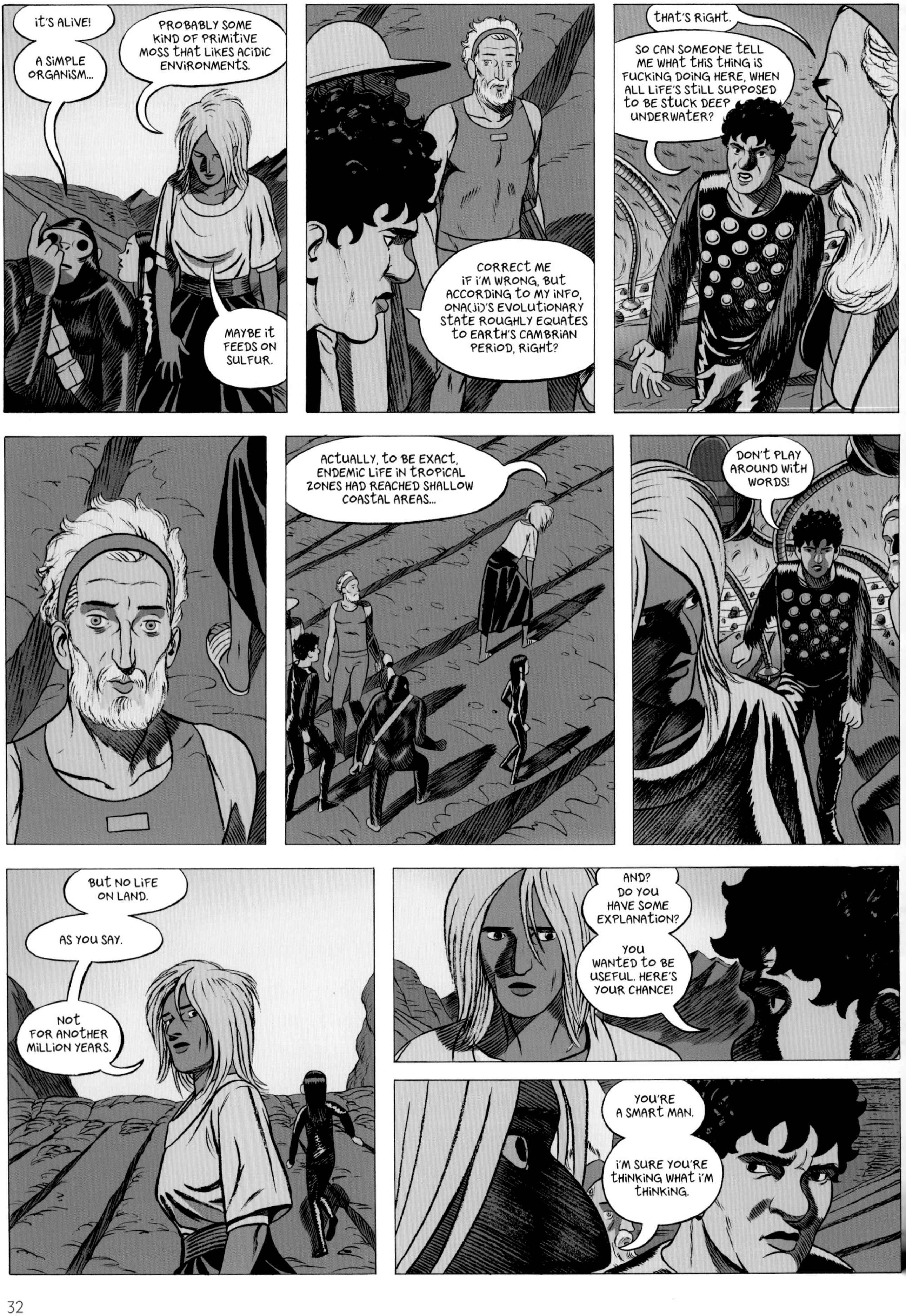
it'S ALiVE!
A SiMPLE ORGANiSM...
PROBABLY SOME KiND OF PRiMitiVE MOSS that LiKES ACiDiC ENViRONMENTS.
MAYBE it FEEDS ON SULFUR.
CORRECT ME iF i'M WRONG, But ACCORDiNG to MY iNFO, ONA(Ji)'S EVOLUtiONARY StAtE ROUGHLY EQUAtES to EARtH'S CAMBRiAN PERiOD, RiGHt?
tHAt'S RiGHt.
SO CAN SOMEONE tELL ME WHAt tHiS tHiNG iS FUCKiNG DOiNG HERE, WHEN ALL LiFE'S StiLL SUPPOSED to BE StUCK DEEP UNDERWAtER?
ACtUALLY, to BE EXACt, ENDEMiC LiFE iN tROPiCAL ZONES HAD REACHED SHALLOW COAStAL AREAS...
DON't PLAY AROUND WitH WORDS!
But NO LiFE ON LAND.
AS YOU SAY.
Not FOR ANOtHER MiLLiON YEARS.
AND? DO YOU HAVE SOME EXPLANAtiON?
YOU WANtED to BE USEFUL. HERE'S YOUR CHANCE!
YOU'RE A SMARt MAN.
i'M SURE YOU'RE tHiNKiNG WHAt i'M tHiNKiNG.

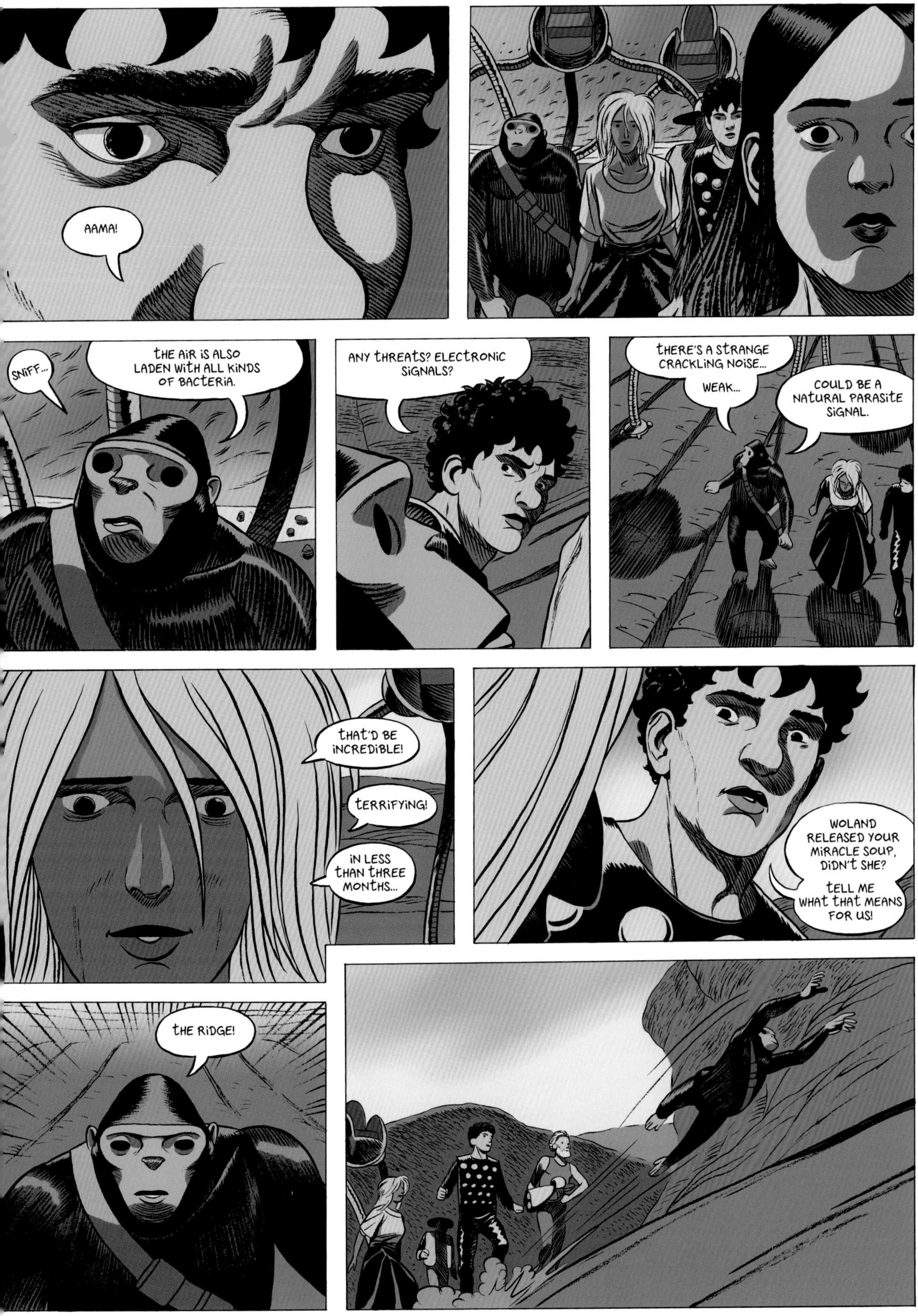

AAMA!
SNIFF...
THE AIR IS ALSO LADEN WITH ALL KINDS OF BACTERIA.
ANY THREATS? ELECTRONIC SIGNALS?
THERE'S A STRANGE CRACKLING NOISE...
WEAK...
COULD BE A NATURAL PARASITE SIGNAL.
THAT'D BE INCREDIBLE!
TERRIFYING!
IN LESS THAN THREE MONTHS...
WOLAND RELEASED YOUR MIRACLE SOUP, DIDN'T SHE?
TELL ME WHAT THAT MEANS FOR US!
THE RIDGE!

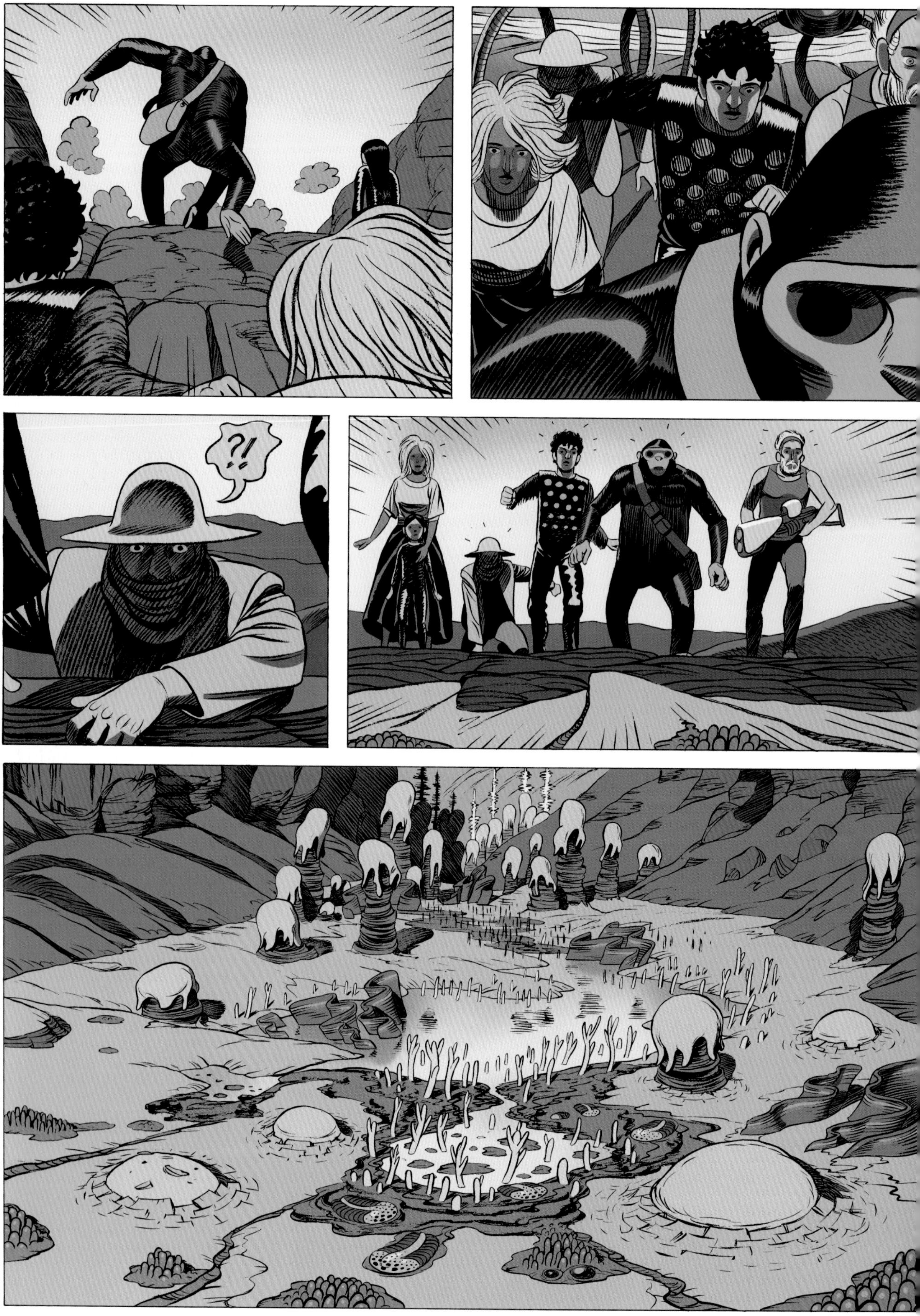
?!

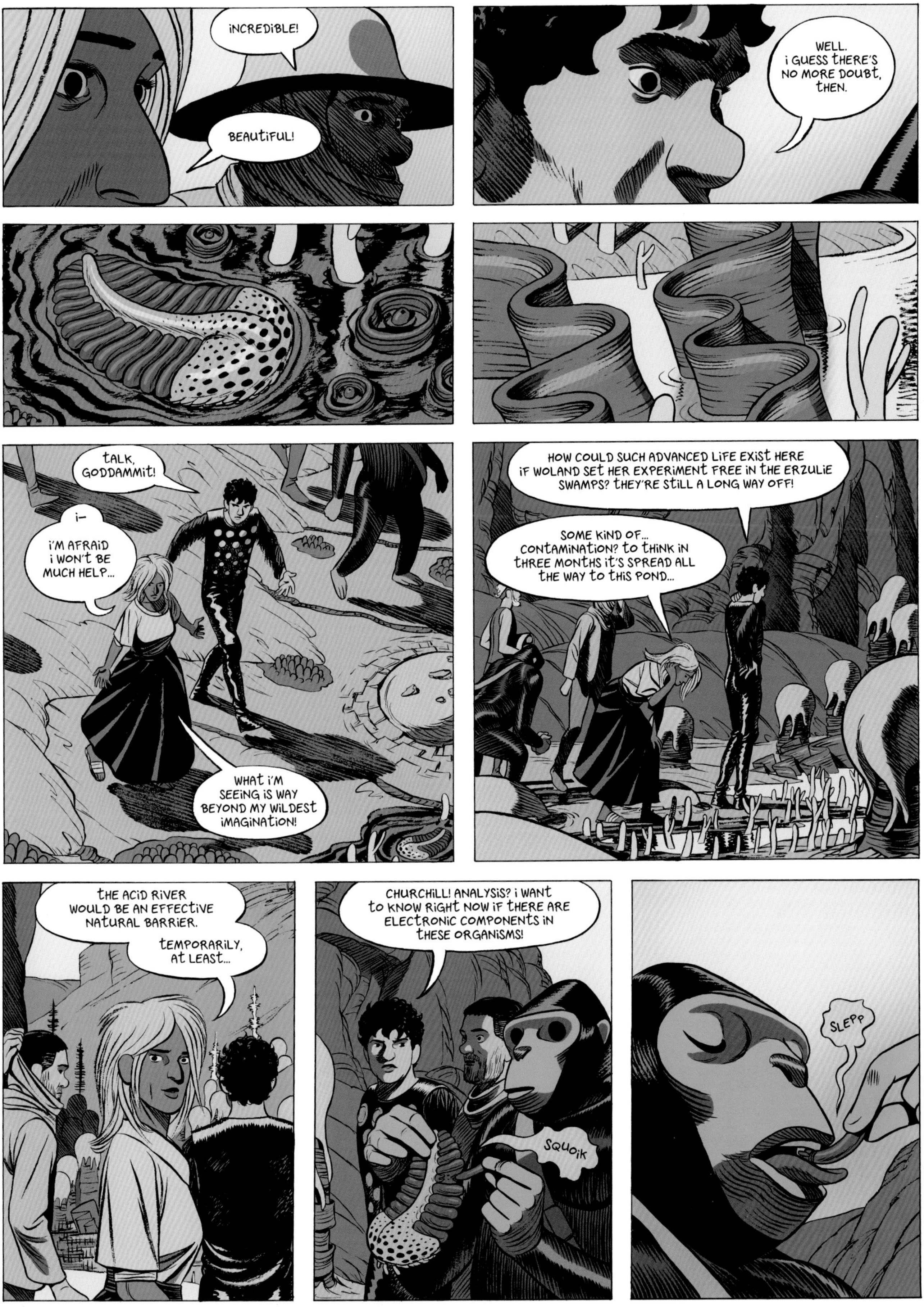
iNCREDIBLE!
BEAUtiFUL!
WELL. i GUESS tHERE'S NO MORE DOUBt, tHEN.
tALK, GODDAMMit!
i–
i'M AFRAiD i WON'T BE MUCH HELP...
WHAt i'M SEEiNG iS WAY BEYOND MY WiLDESt iMAGiNAtiON!
HOW COULD SUCH ADVANCED LiFE EXiSt HERE iF WOLAND SEt HER EXPERiMENt FREE iN tHE ERZULiE SWAMPS? tHEY'RE StiLL A LONG WAY OFF!
SOME KiND OF... CONtAMiNAtiON? tO tHiNK iN tHREE MONtHS it'S SPREAD ALL tHE WAY tO tHiS POND...
tHE ACiD RiVER WOULD BE AN EFFECtiVE NAtURAL BARRiER.
tEMPORARiLY, At LEASt...
CHURCHiLL! ANALYSiS? i WANt tO KNOW RiGHt NOW iF tHERE ARE ELECtRONiC COMPONENtS iN tHESE ORGANiSMS!
SQUOiK
SLEPP

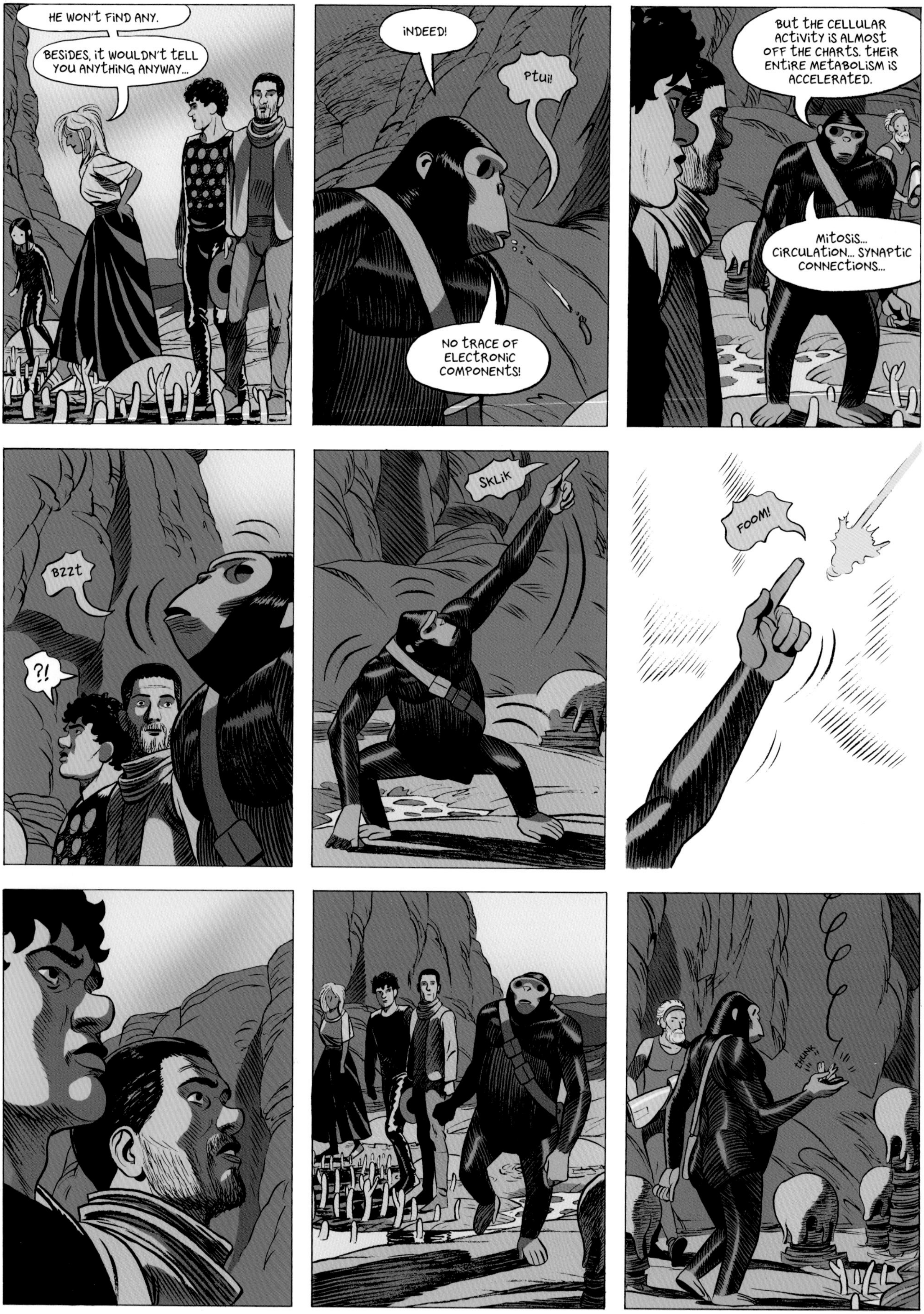
HE WON'T FIND ANY.
BESIDES, IT WOULDN'T TELL YOU ANYTHING ANYWAY...
INDEED!
PTUI!
NO TRACE OF ELECTRONIC COMPONENTS!
BUT THE CELLULAR ACTIVITY IS ALMOST OFF THE CHARTS. THEIR ENTIRE METABOLISM IS ACCELERATED.
MITOSIS... CIRCULATION... SYNAPTIC CONNECTIONS...
BZZT
?!
SKLIK
FOOM!
THUNK

A ROBOT?

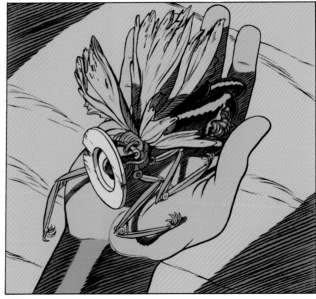

SOME KIND OF DRONE...
A HYBRID...
HALF-ORGANIC.

LOOKS LIKE THE WINGS AND INTESTINES GRAFTED ONTO A VISION MODULE FROM ONE OF THE COLONY ROBOTS!

IT'S COMPLETELY MONSTROUS!

ONE THING'S FOR SURE: THEY'RE STILL WATCHING US!

OK. TIME OUT! YOU'RE GOING TO STOP BEATING AROUND THE BUSH AND TELL ME WHAT'S OUT THERE.

OW! YOU'RE HURTING ME!

MY HANDWRITING IS GETTING SUPPLE AND PRECISE — FASTER, EVEN, AS EVENTS SPEED UP. I'M TAKING MORE NOTES.

I'M ALMOST JOTTING DOWN MYO'S EXPLANATIONS IN REAL TIME...

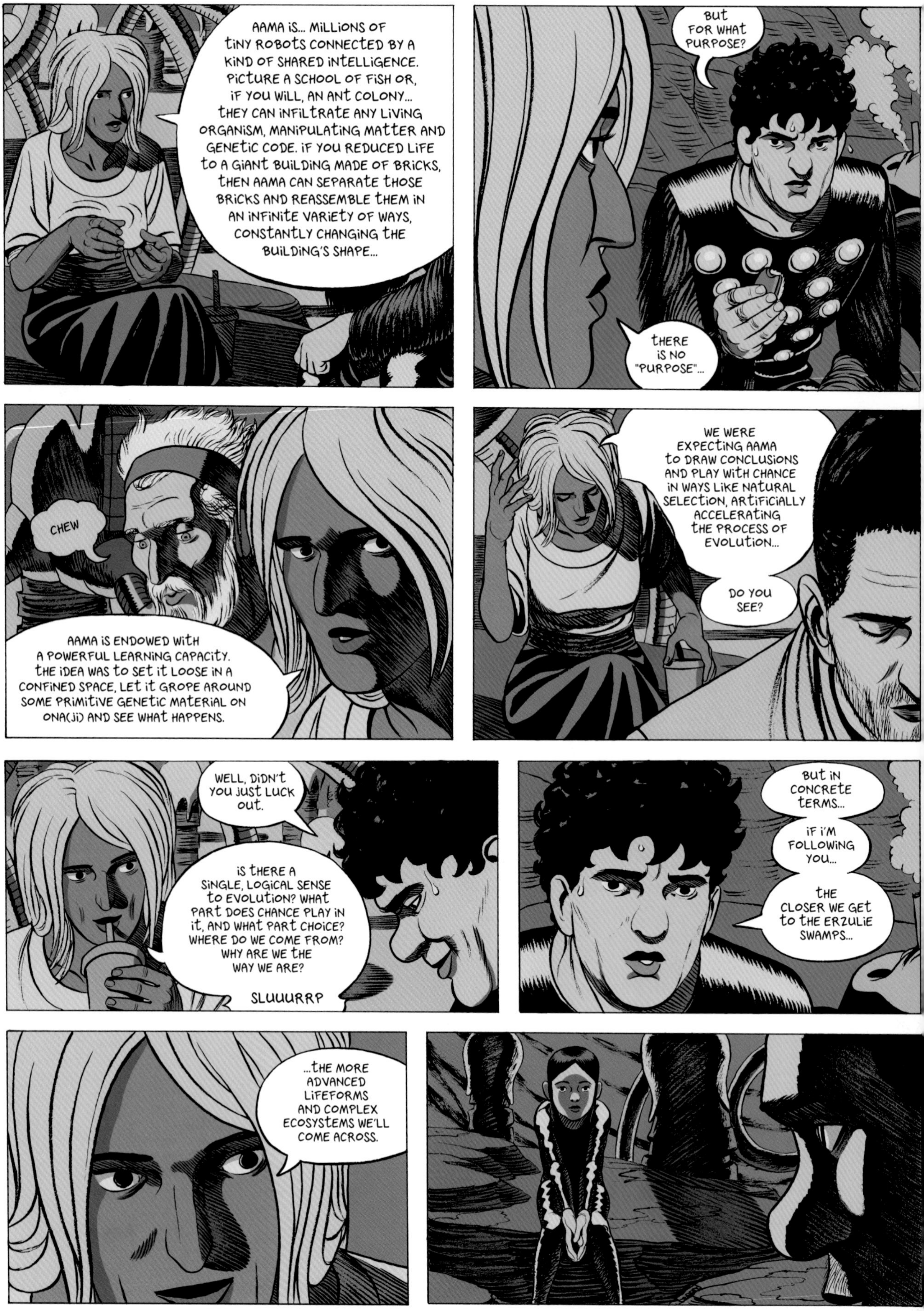
AAMA IS... MILLIONS OF TINY ROBOTS CONNECTED BY A KIND OF SHARED INTELLIGENCE. PICTURE A SCHOOL OF FISH OR, IF YOU WILL, AN ANT COLONY... THEY CAN INFILTRATE ANY LIVING ORGANISM, MANIPULATING MATTER AND GENETIC CODE. IF YOU REDUCED LIFE TO A GIANT BUILDING MADE OF BRICKS, THEN AAMA CAN SEPARATE THOSE BRICKS AND REASSEMBLE THEM IN AN INFINITE VARIETY OF WAYS, CONSTANTLY CHANGING THE BUILDING'S SHAPE...
BUT FOR WHAT PURPOSE?
THERE IS NO "PURPOSE"...
CHEW
AAMA IS ENDOWED WITH A POWERFUL LEARNING CAPACITY. THE IDEA WAS TO SET IT LOOSE IN A CONFINED SPACE, LET IT GROPE AROUND SOME PRIMITIVE GENETIC MATERIAL ON ONA(JI) AND SEE WHAT HAPPENS.
WE WERE EXPECTING AAMA TO DRAW CONCLUSIONS AND PLAY WITH CHANCE IN WAYS LIKE NATURAL SELECTION, ARTIFICIALLY ACCELERATING THE PROCESS OF EVOLUTION...
DO YOU SEE?
WELL, DIDN'T YOU JUST LUCK OUT.
IS THERE A SINGLE, LOGICAL SENSE TO EVOLUTION? WHAT PART DOES CHANCE PLAY IN IT, AND WHAT PART CHOICE? WHERE DO WE COME FROM? WHY ARE WE THE WAY WE ARE?
SLUUURRP
BUT IN CONCRETE TERMS...
IF I'M FOLLOWING YOU...
THE CLOSER WE GET TO THE ERZULIE SWAMPS...
...THE MORE ADVANCED LIFEFORMS AND COMPLEX ECOSYSTEMS WE'LL COME ACROSS.

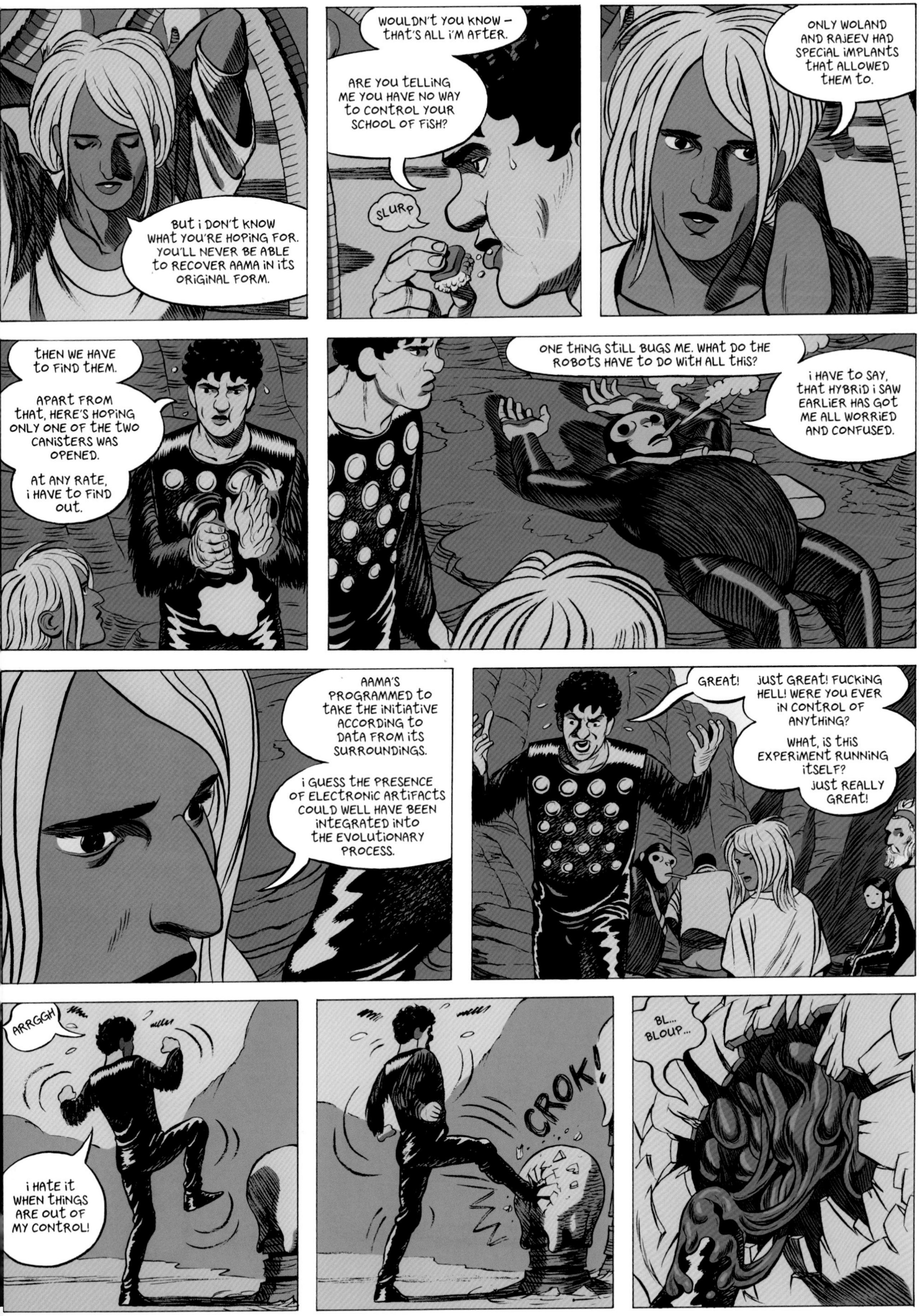

But i DON'T KNOW WHAT YOU'RE HOPING FOR. YOU'LL NEVER BE ABLE to RECOVER AAMA IN its ORIGINAL FORM.
WOULDN'T YOU KNOW – THAT'S ALL I'M AFTER.
ARE YOU TELLING ME YOU HAVE NO WAY to CONTROL YOUR SCHOOL OF FISH?
SLURP
ONLY WOLAND AND RAJEEV HAD SPECIAL IMPLANTS THAT ALLOWED THEM TO.
THEN WE HAVE TO FIND THEM.
APART FROM THAT, HERE'S HOPING ONLY ONE OF THE TWO CANISTERS WAS OPENED.
AT ANY RATE, I HAVE TO FIND OUT.
ONE THING STILL BUGS ME. WHAT DO THE ROBOTS HAVE TO DO WITH ALL THIS?
I HAVE TO SAY, THAT HYBRID I SAW EARLIER HAS GOT ME ALL WORRIED AND CONFUSED.
AAMA'S PROGRAMMED TO TAKE THE INITIATIVE ACCORDING TO DATA FROM ITS SURROUNDINGS.
I GUESS THE PRESENCE OF ELECTRONIC ARTIFACTS COULD WELL HAVE BEEN INTEGRATED INTO THE EVOLUTIONARY PROCESS.
GREAT!
JUST GREAT! FUCKING HELL! WERE YOU EVER IN CONTROL OF ANYTHING?
WHAT, IS THIS EXPERIMENT RUNNING ITSELF?
JUST REALLY GREAT!
ARRGGH
I HATE IT WHEN THINGS ARE OUT OF MY CONTROL!
CROK!
BL... BLOUP...

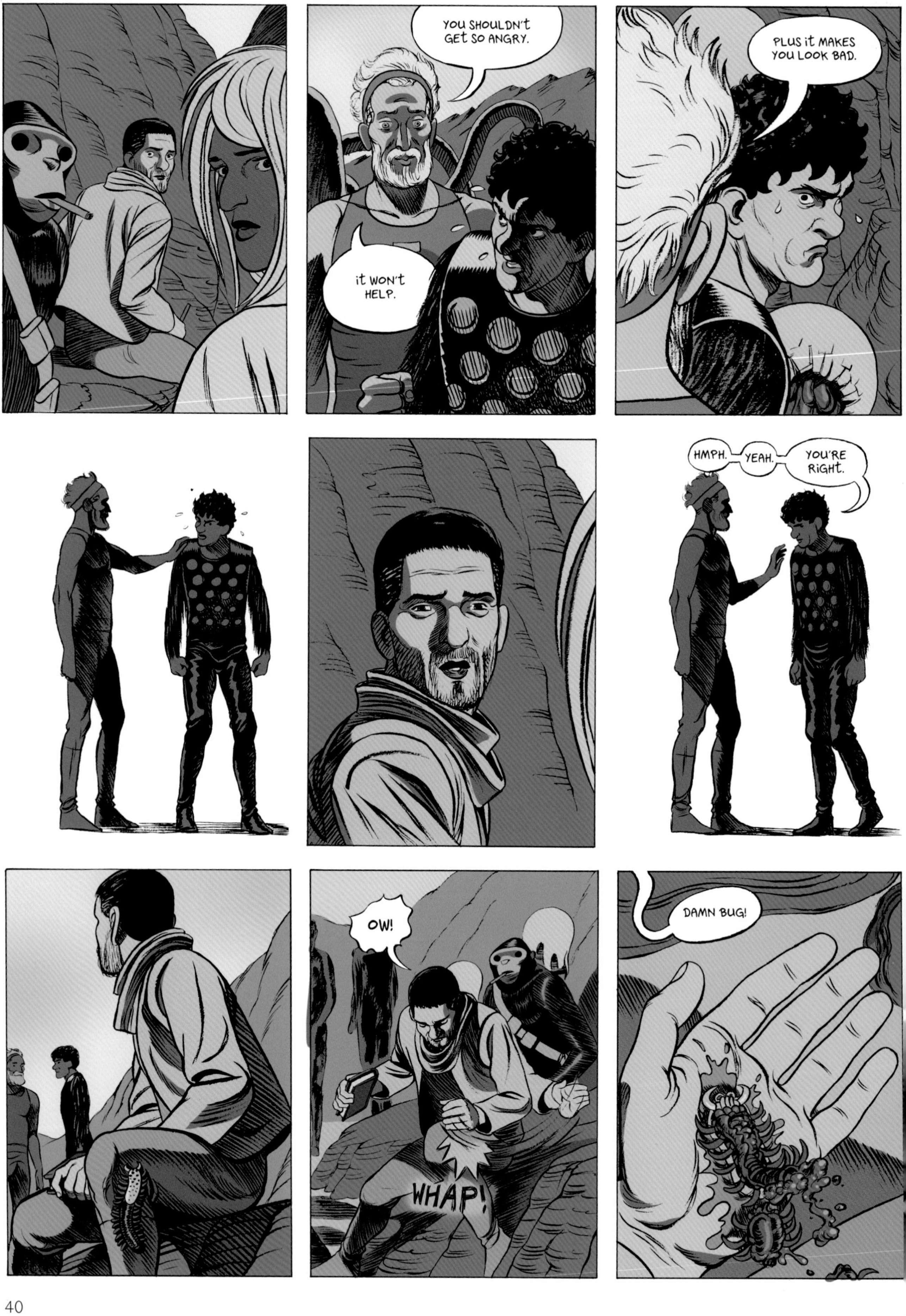
YOU SHOULDN'T GET SO ANGRY.
it WON'T HELP.
PLUS it MAKES YOU LOOK BAD.
HMPH.
YEAH.
YOU'RE RIGHT.
OW!
WHAP!
DAMN BUG!

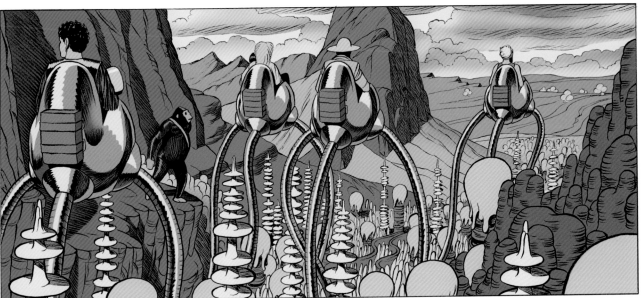

NATURE HAS NO LOVE FOR MAN.

HOW WELL i KNOW it. it's SOMETHING MY BOOKS HAVE TAUGHT ME.

CENTURIES OF ENMITY AND STRUGGLE FOR SURVIVAL.

BUT i WAS BORN ON RADIANT.

AND SO, DESPITE MYSELF, i BUILT UP AN ALMOST MYTHIC IMAGE OF THE NATURAL WORLD: ONE OF CALMING BEAUTY, COMMUNION AND REJUVENATING PURITY.

LIKE EVERY HUMAN, DEEP DOWN iN MY REPTiLiAN BRAiN i HAVE A VAGUE NOSTALGiA FOR A NATURAL WORLD i'VE NEVER KNOWN.

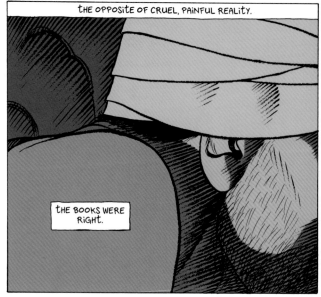

THE OPPOSITE OF CRUEL, PAINFUL REALITY.

THE BOOKS WERE RiGHT.

42

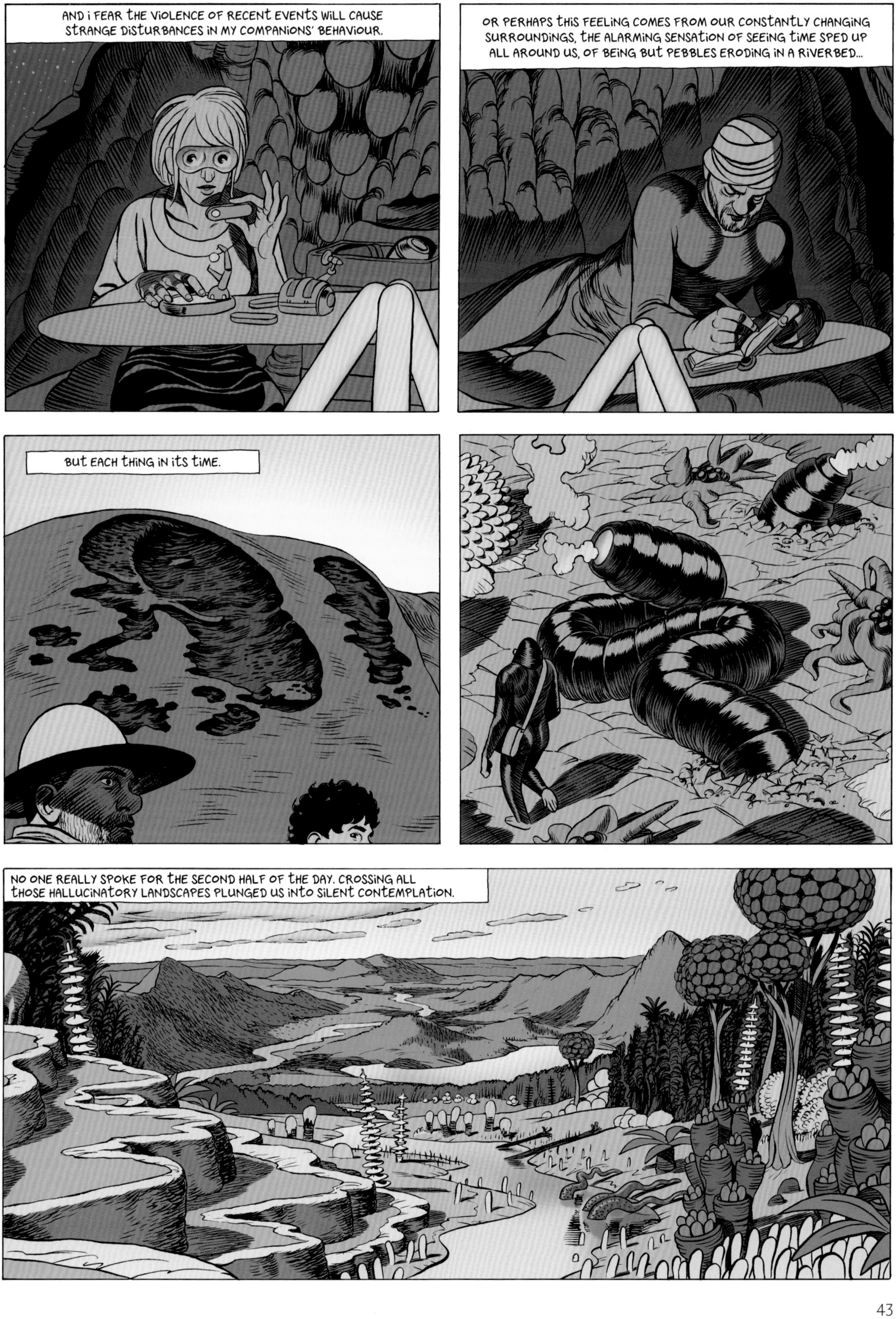
AND I FEAR THE VIOLENCE OF RECENT EVENTS WILL CAUSE STRANGE DISTURBANCES IN MY COMPANIONS' BEHAVIOUR.
OR PERHAPS THIS FEELING COMES FROM OUR CONSTANTLY CHANGING SURROUNDINGS, THE ALARMING SENSATION OF SEEING TIME SPED UP ALL AROUND US, OF BEING BUT PEBBLES ERODING IN A RIVERBED...
BUT EACH THING IN ITS TIME.
NO ONE REALLY SPOKE FOR THE SECOND HALF OF THE DAY. CROSSING ALL THOSE HALLUCINATORY LANDSCAPES PLUNGED US INTO SILENT CONTEMPLATION.

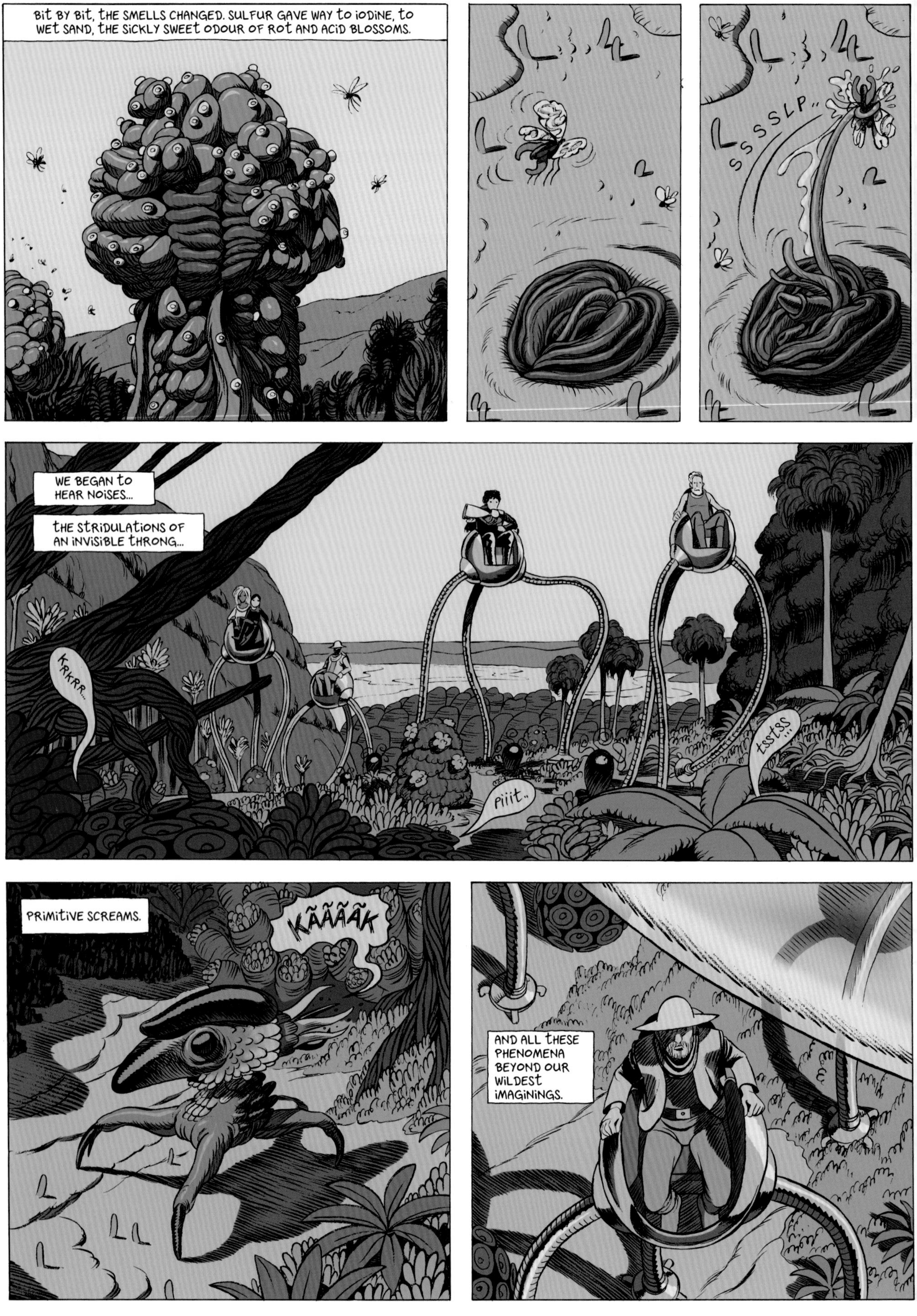
BIT BY BIT, THE SMELLS CHANGED. SULFUR GAVE WAY TO IODINE, TO WET SAND, THE SICKLY SWEET ODOUR OF ROT AND ACID BLOSSOMS.
SSSSLP..
WE BEGAN TO HEAR NOISES...
THE STRIDULATIONS OF AN INVISIBLE THRONG...
KRKRR...
PIIIT..
TSSTSS...
PRIMITIVE SCREAMS.
KÃÃÃÃK
AND ALL THESE PHENOMENA BEYOND OUR WILDEST IMAGININGS.

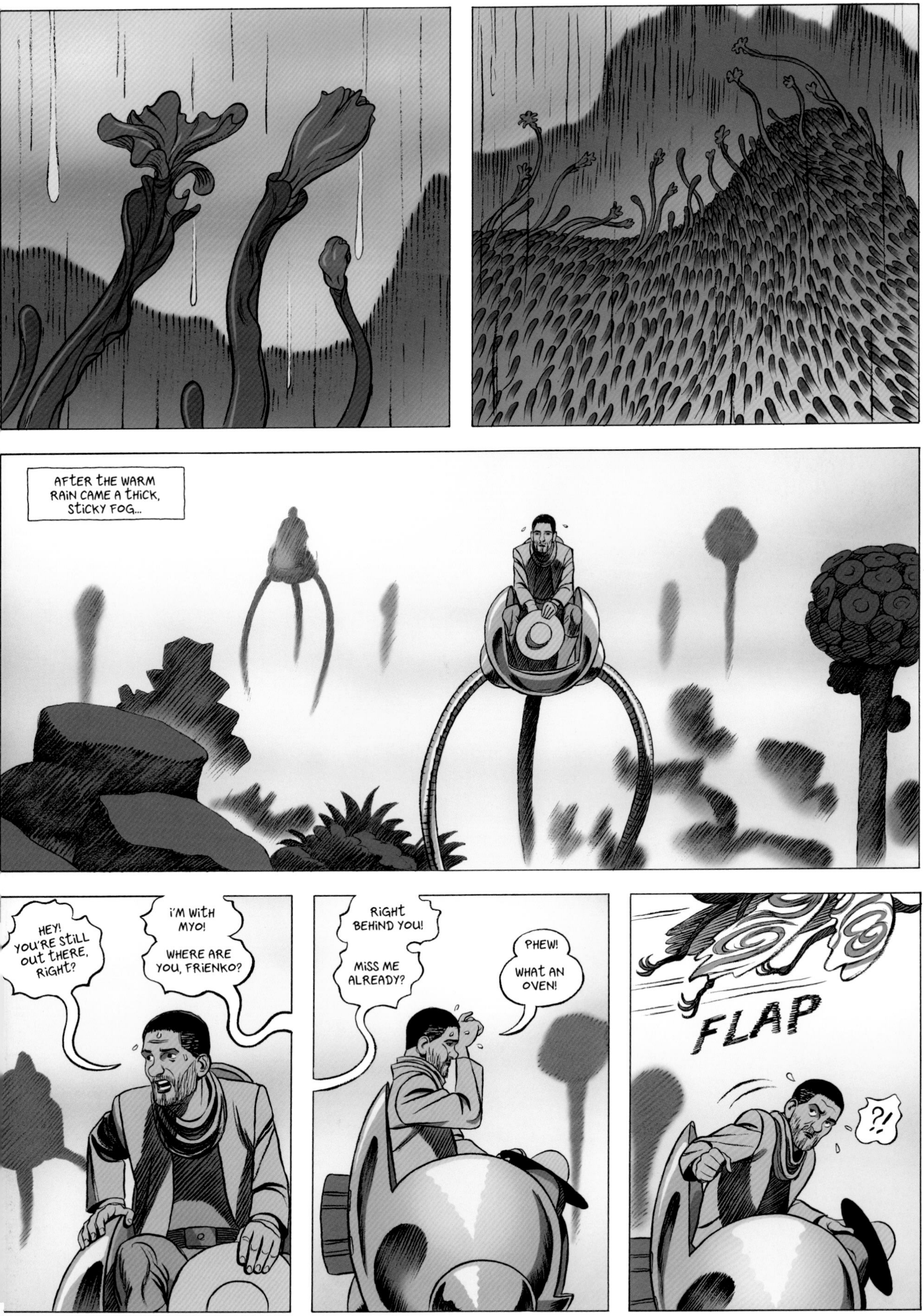
AFTER THE WARM RAIN CAME A THICK, STICKY FOG...
HEY! YOU'RE STILL OUT THERE, RIGHT?
I'M WITH MYO!
WHERE ARE YOU, FRIENKO?
RIGHT BEHIND YOU!
MISS ME ALREADY?
PHEW!
WHAT AN OVEN!
FLAP
?!

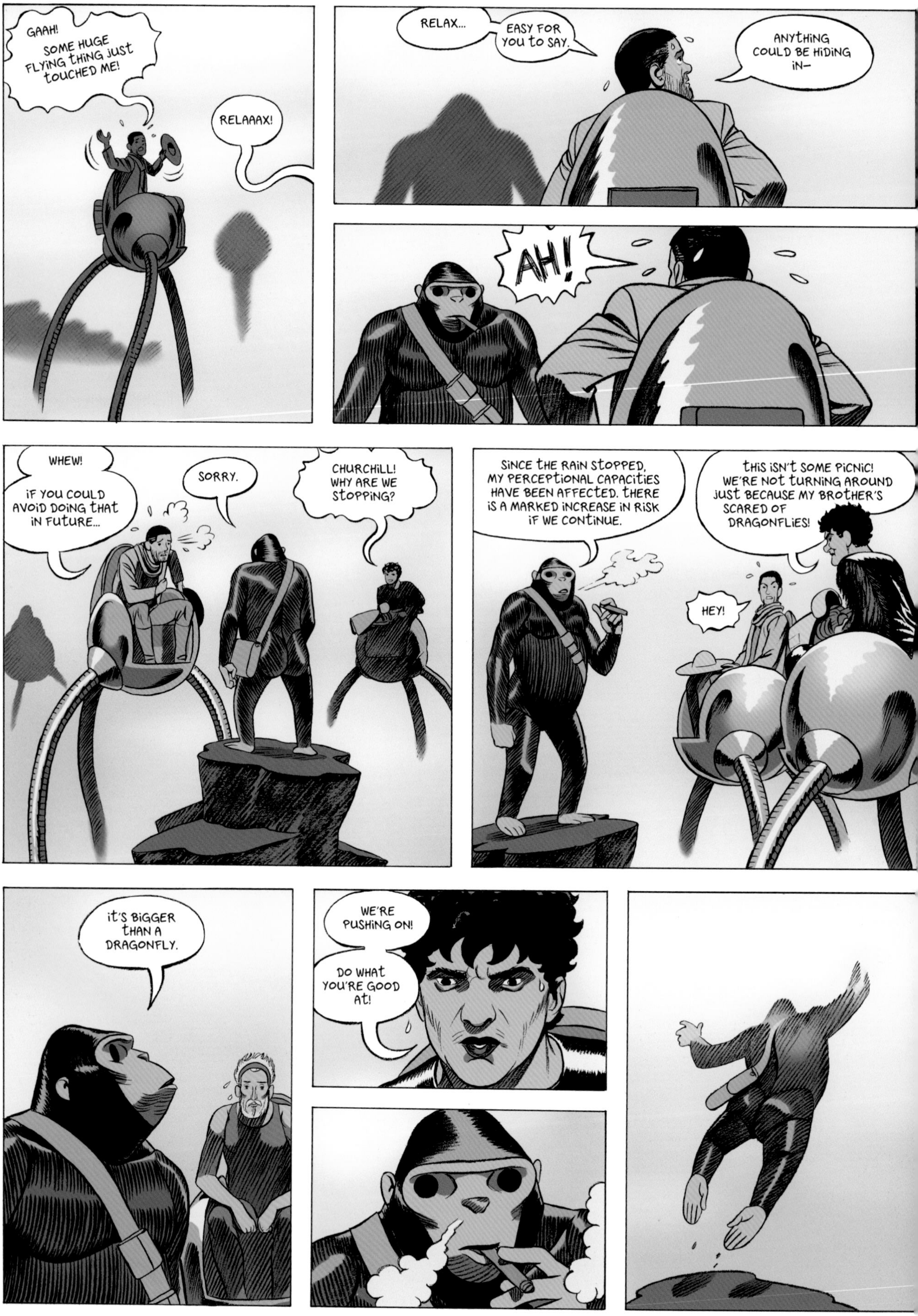
GAAH!
SOME HUGE FLYING THING JUST TOUCHED ME!
RELAAAX!
RELAX...
EASY FOR YOU TO SAY.
ANYTHING COULD BE HIDING IN–
AH!
WHEW!
IF YOU COULD AVOID DOING THAT IN FUTURE...
SORRY.
CHURCHILL! WHY ARE WE STOPPING?
SINCE THE RAIN STOPPED, MY PERCEPTIONAL CAPACITIES HAVE BEEN AFFECTED. THERE IS A MARKED INCREASE IN RISK IF WE CONTINUE.
THIS ISN'T SOME PICNIC! WE'RE NOT TURNING AROUND JUST BECAUSE MY BROTHER'S SCARED OF DRAGONFLIES!
HEY!
IT'S BIGGER THAN A DRAGONFLY.
WE'RE PUSHING ON!
DO WHAT YOU'RE GOOD AT!

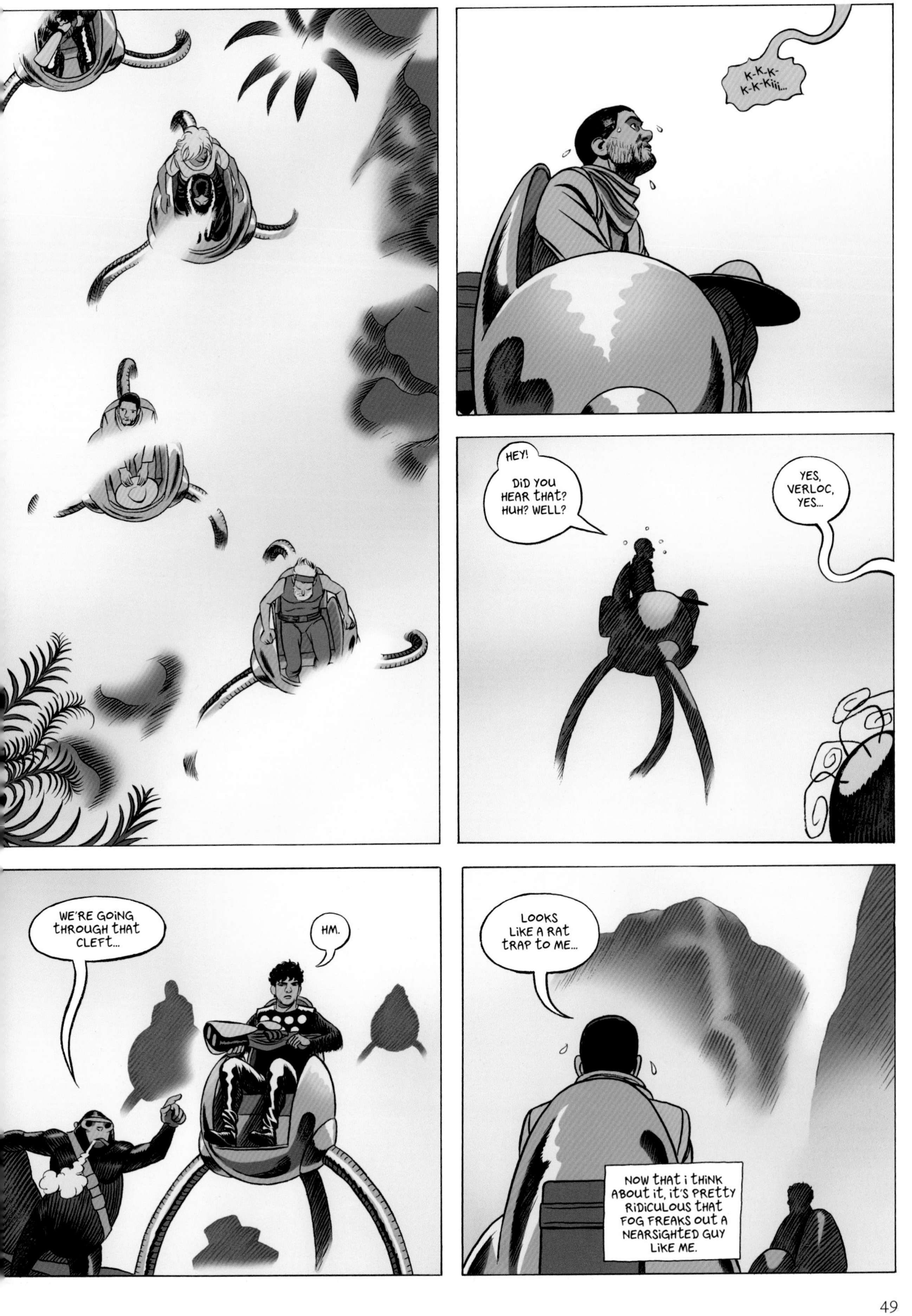
K-K-K-
K-K-Kiii...
HEY!
DiD YOU HEAR thAt? HUH? WELL?
YES, VERLOC, YES...
WE'RE GOiNG thROUGH thAt CLEFt...
HM.
LOOKS LiKE A RAt tRAP tO ME...
NOW thAt i thiNK ABOUt it, it'S PREttY RiDiCULOUS thAt FOG FREAKS OUt A NEARSiGhtED GUY LiKE ME.

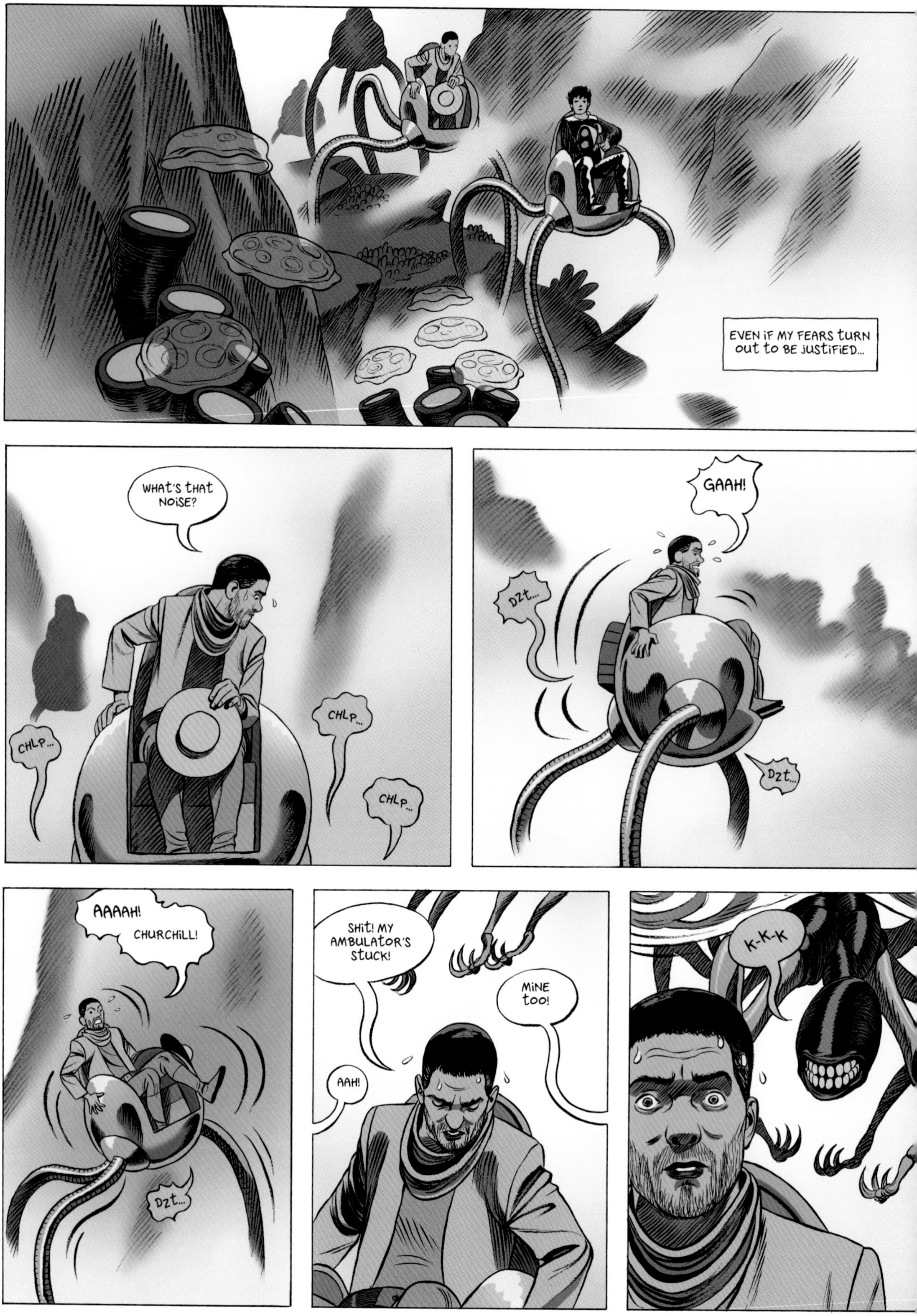

EVEN IF MY FEARS TURN OUT TO BE JUSTIFIED...
WHAT'S THAT NOISE?
CHLP...
CHLP...
CHLP...
GAAH!
DZT...
DZT...
AAAAH!
CHURCHILL!
DZT...
SHIT! MY AMBULATOR'S STUCK!
AAH!
MINE TOO!
K-K-K

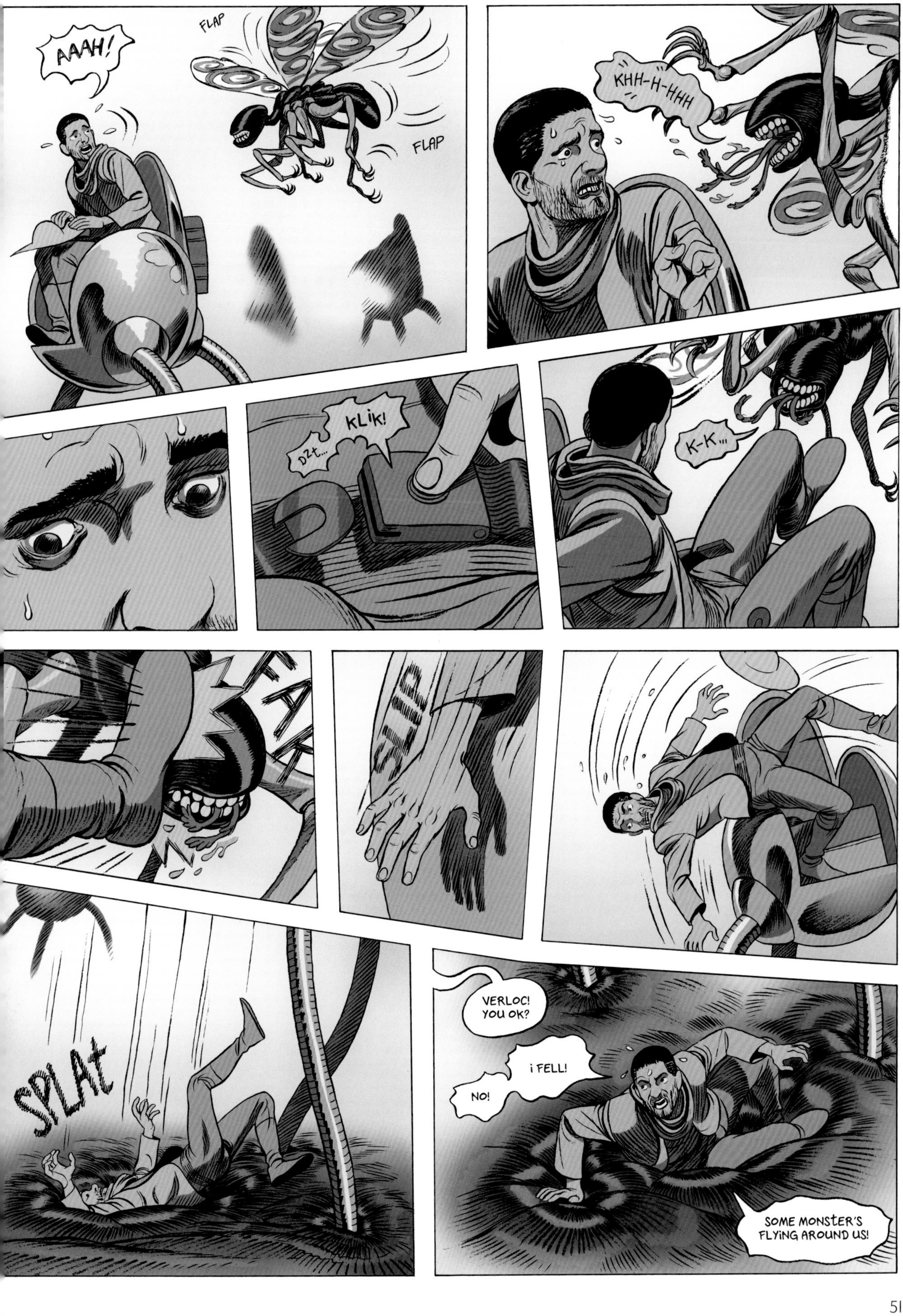
AAAH!
FLAP
FLAP
KHH-H-HHH
DZt...
KLiK!
K-K...
FAK
SLIP
SPLAt
VERLOC! YOU OK?
¡ FELL!
NO!
SOME MONSTER'S FLYiNG AROUND US!

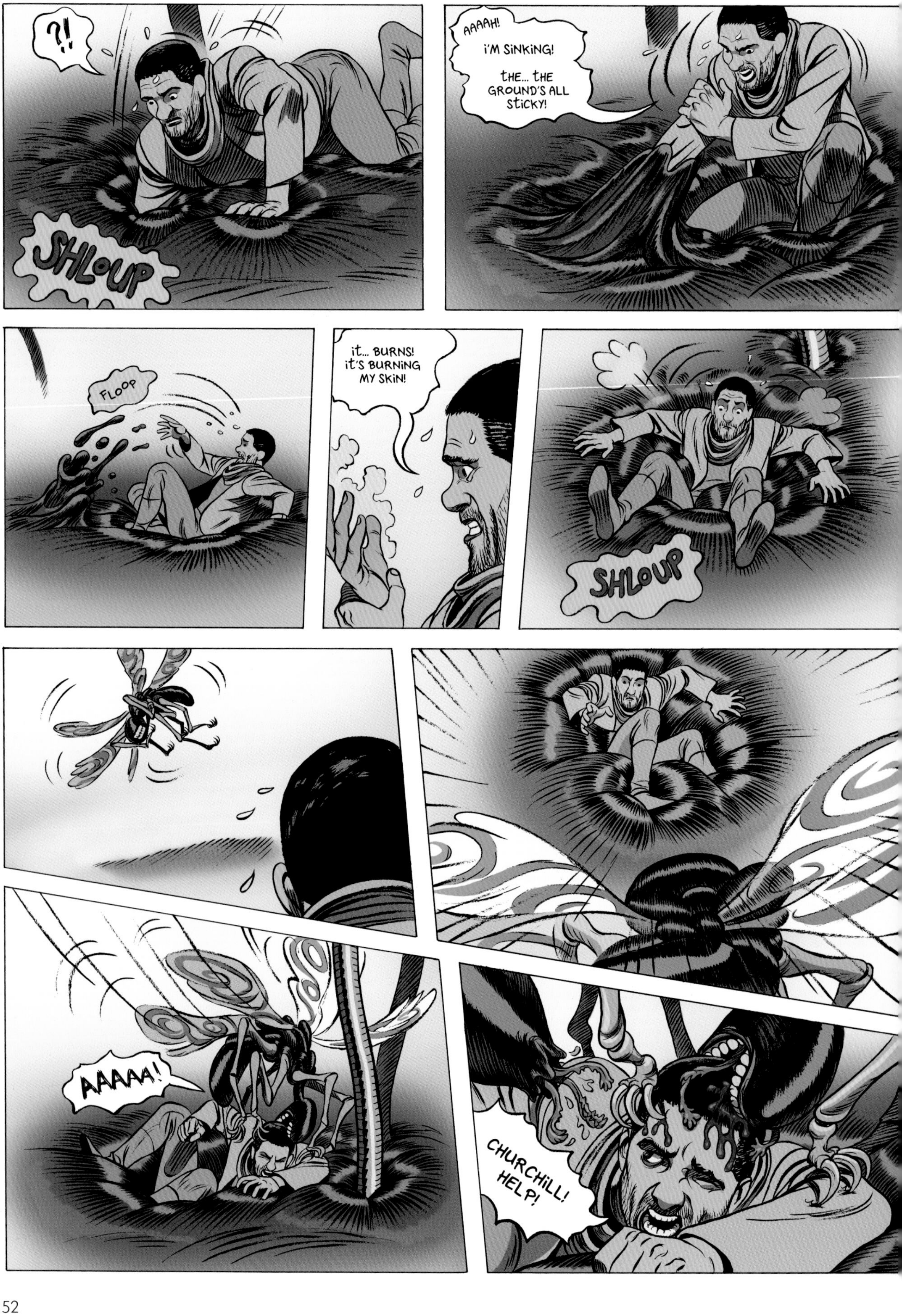
?!
SHLOUP
AAAAH!
I'M SINKING!
THE... THE GROUND'S ALL STICKY!
FLOOP
IT... BURNS! IT'S BURNING MY SKIN!
SHLOUP
AAAAA!
CHURCHILL! HELP!

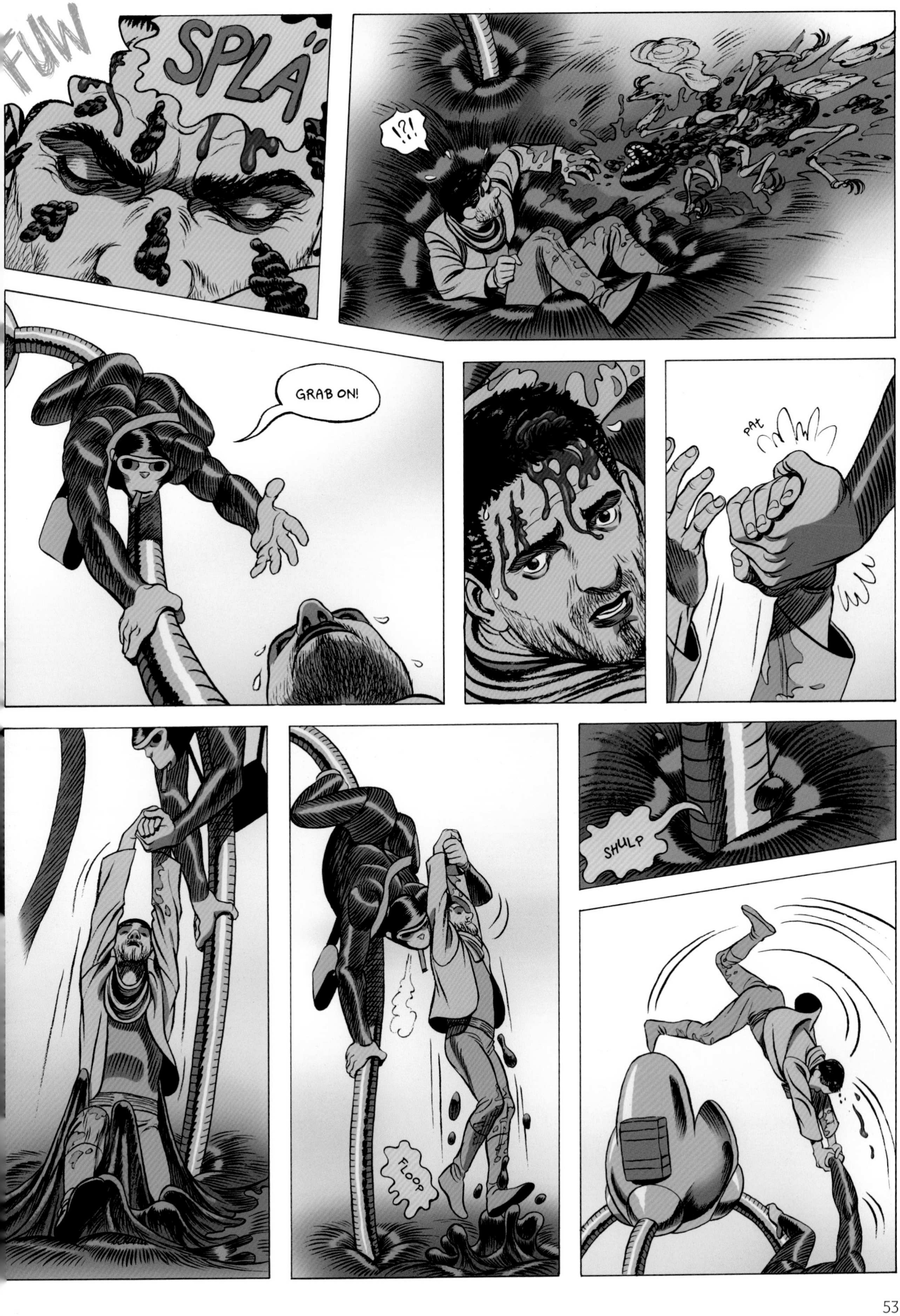
FUW
SPLÄ
!?!
GRAB ON!
PAT
SHULP
FLOOP

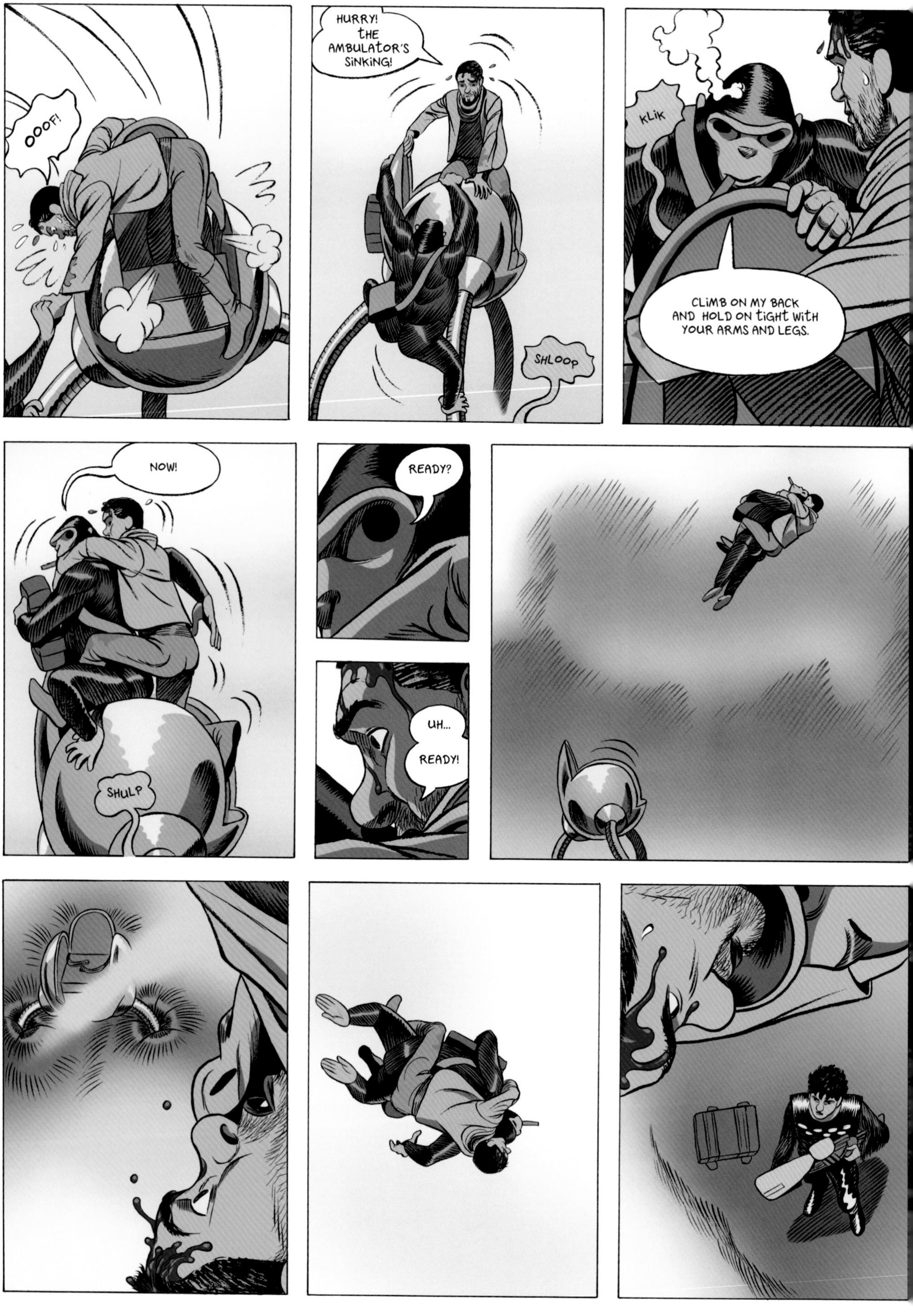
OOOF!
HURRY! THE AMBULATOR'S SINKING!
SHLOOP
KLIK
CLIMB ON MY BACK AND HOLD ON TIGHT WITH YOUR ARMS AND LEGS.
NOW!
SHULP
READY?
UH... READY!

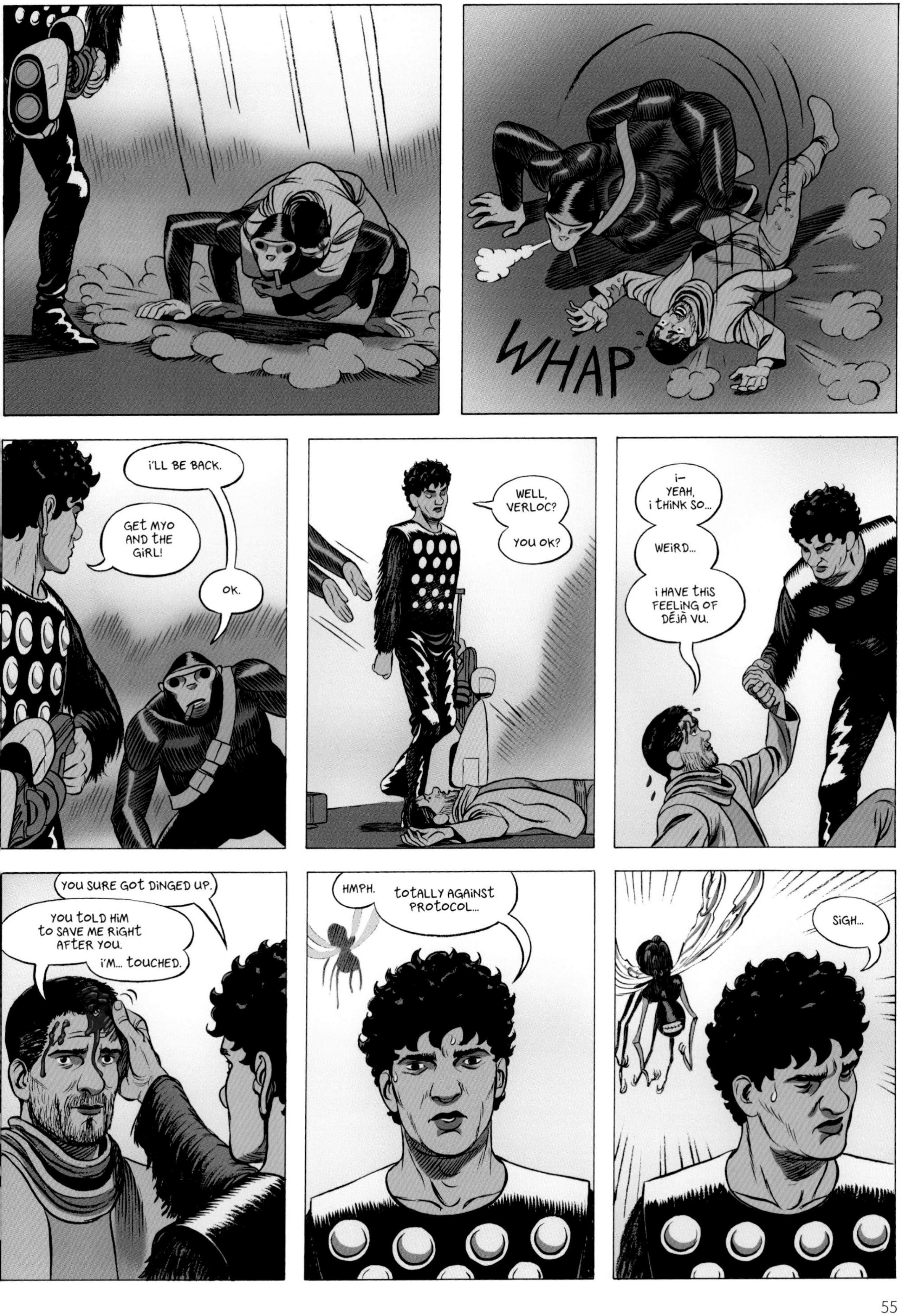
WHAP
i'LL BE BACK.
GEt MYO AND tHE GiRL!
OK.
WELL, VERLOC?
YOU OK?
i— YEAH, i tHiNK SO...
WEiRD...
i HAVE tHiS FEELiNG OF DÉJÀ VU.
YOU SURE GOt DiNGED UP.
YOU tOLD HiM tO SAVE ME RiGHt AFtER YOU.
i'M... tOUCHED.
HMPH.
tOtALLY AGAiNSt PROtOCOL...
SiGH...

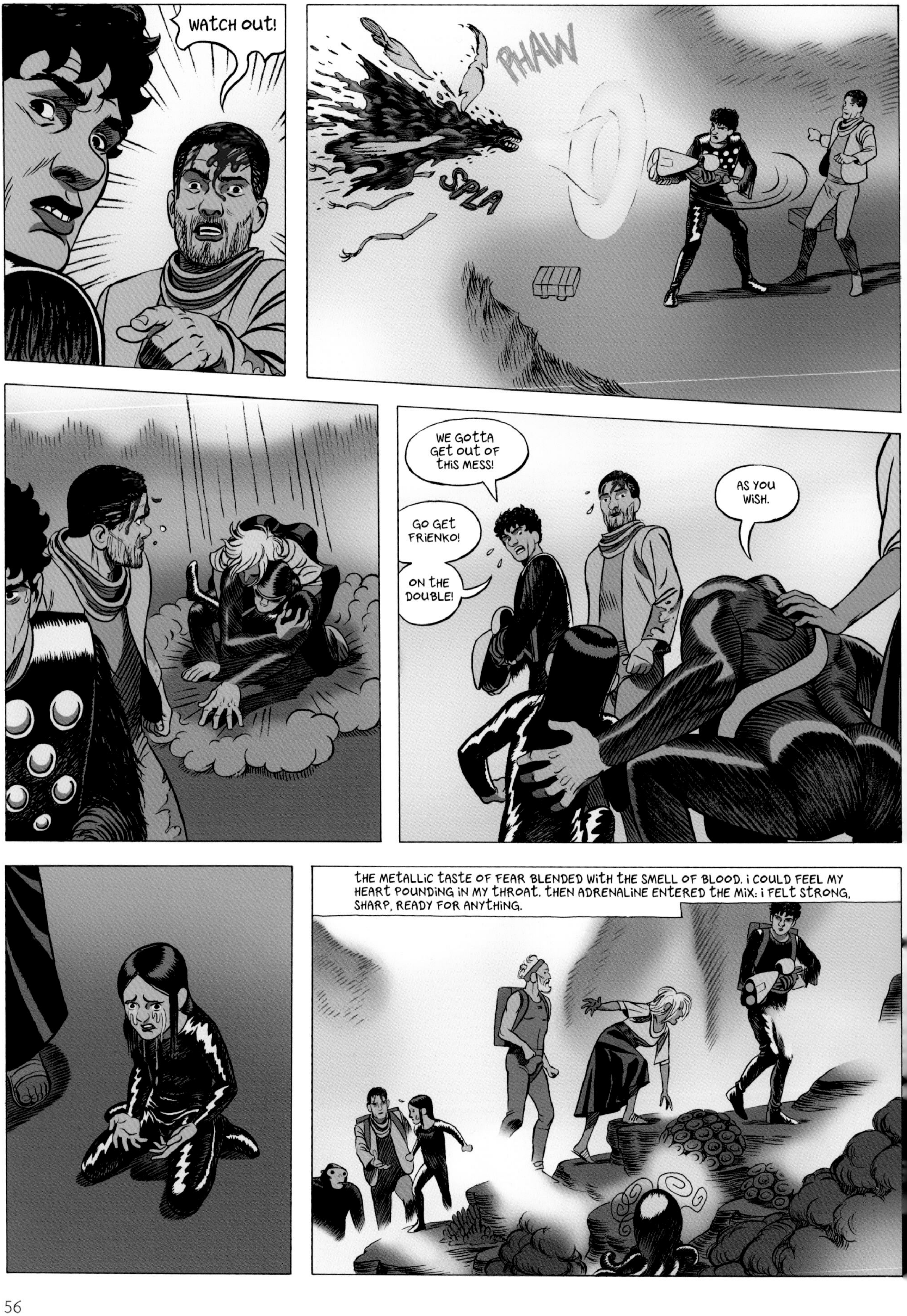
WATCH OUT!
PHAW
SPLA
WE GOTTA GET OUT OF THIS MESS!
GO GET FRIENKO!
ON THE DOUBLE!
AS YOU WISH.
THE METALLIC TASTE OF FEAR BLENDED WITH THE SMELL OF BLOOD. I COULD FEEL MY HEART POUNDING IN MY THROAT. THEN ADRENALINE ENTERED THE MIX: I FELT STRONG, SHARP, READY FOR ANYTHING.

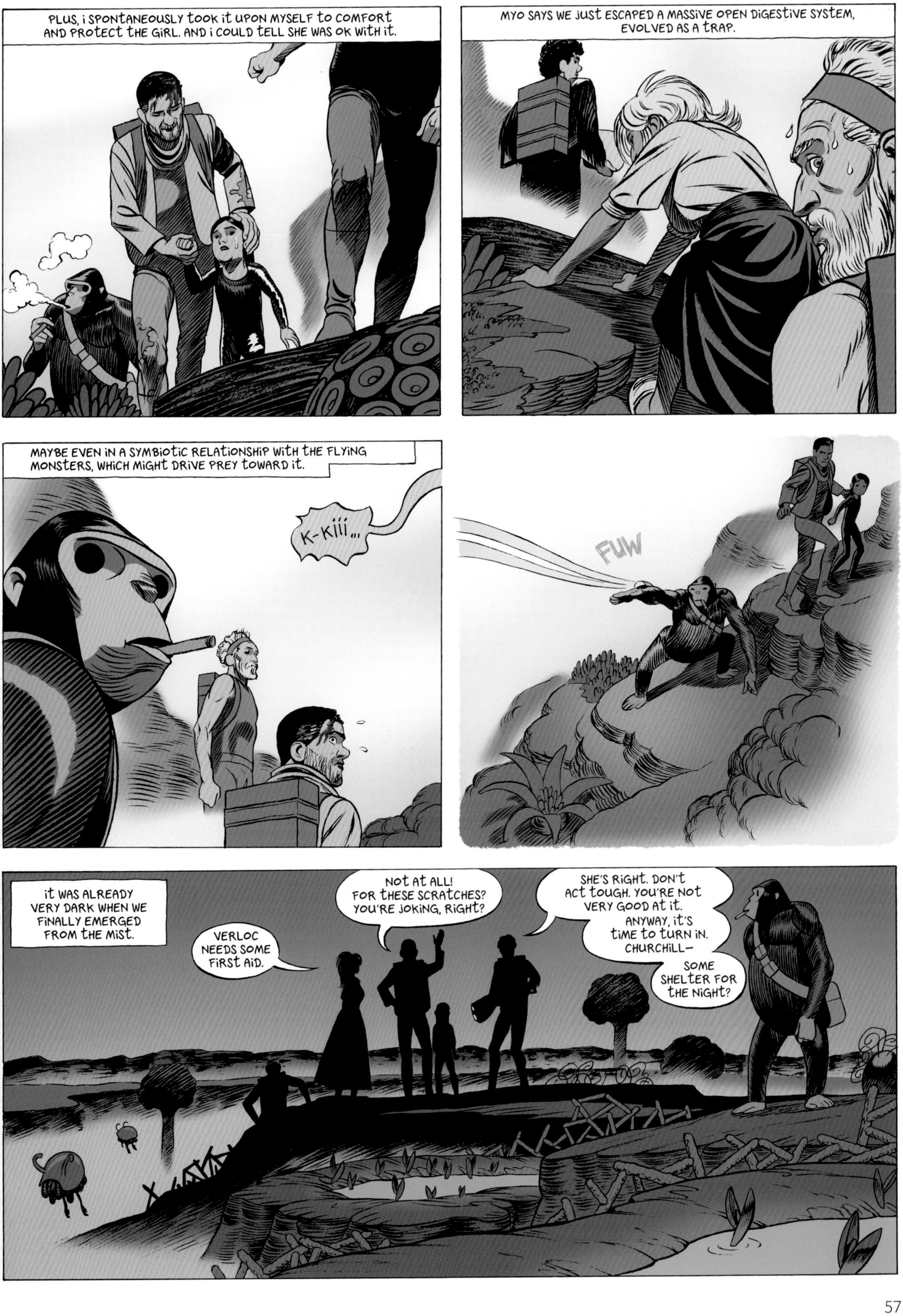

PLUS, i SPONTANEOUSLY took it UPON MYSELF to COMFORT AND PROTECT THE GIRL. AND i COULD TELL SHE WAS OK WITH it.
MYO SAYS WE JUST ESCAPED A MASSIVE OPEN DIGESTIVE SYSTEM, EVOLVED AS A TRAP.
MAYBE EVEN iN A SYMBIOTIC RELATIONSHIP WITH THE FLYING MONSTERS, WHICH MIGHT DRIVE PREY TOWARD iT.
K-Kiii...
FUW
it WAS ALREADY VERY DARK WHEN WE FINALLY EMERGED FROM THE MIST.
VERLOC NEEDS SOME FIRST AiD.
Not At ALL! FOR THESE SCRATCHES? YOU'RE JOKING, RIGHT?
SHE'S RIGHT. DON'T ACT TOUGH. YOU'RE NOT VERY GOOD AT iT.
ANYWAY, iT'S TIME TO TURN IN. CHURCHILL—
SOME SHELTER FOR THE NIGHT?

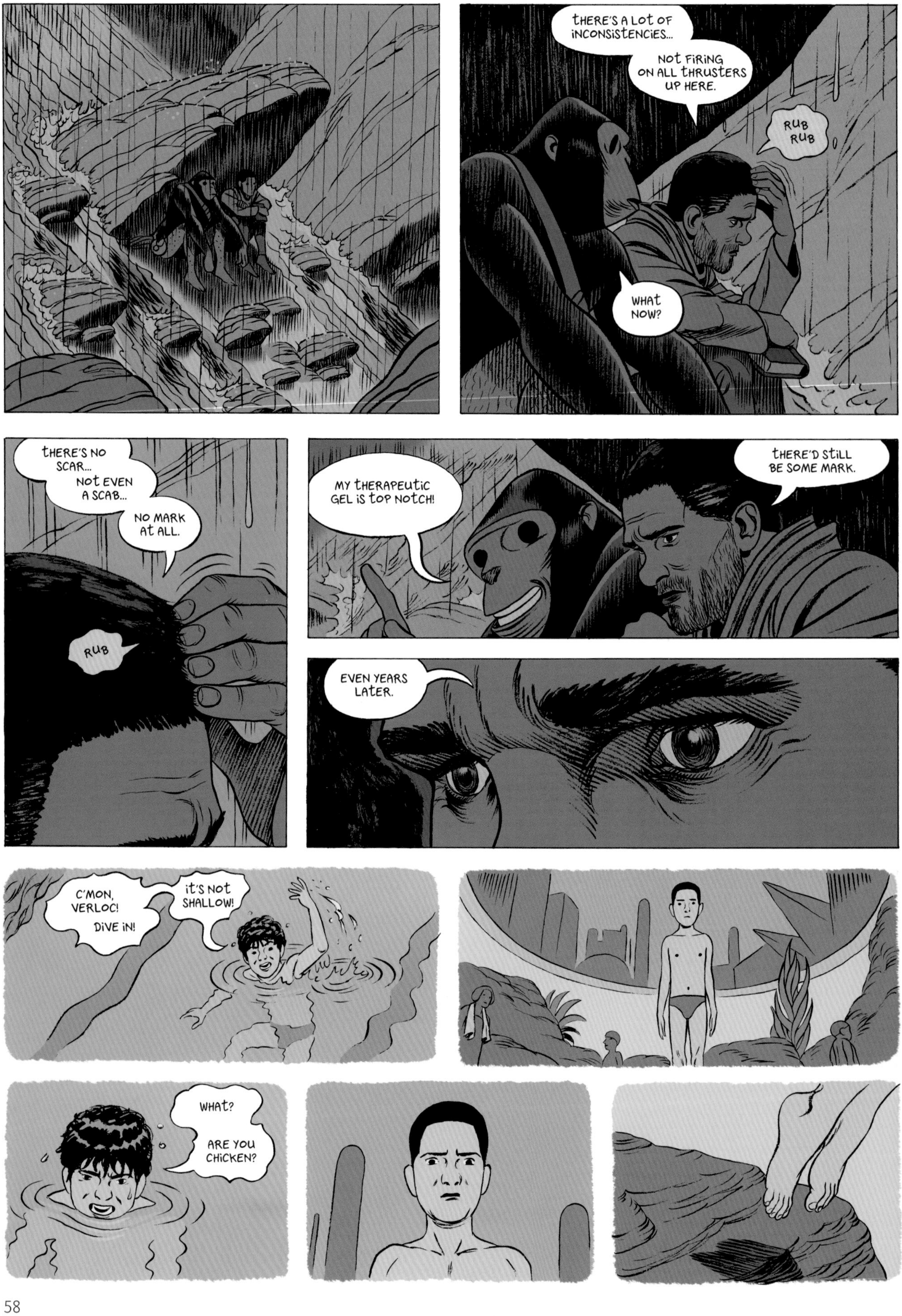

THERE'S A LOT OF INCONSISTENCIES...
NOT FIRING ON ALL THRUSTERS UP HERE.
RUB RUB
WHAT NOW?
THERE'S NO SCAR...
NOT EVEN A SCAB...
NO MARK AT ALL.
RUB
MY THERAPEUTIC GEL IS TOP NOTCH!
THERE'D STILL BE SOME MARK.
EVEN YEARS LATER.
C'MON, VERLOC!
DIVE IN!
IT'S NOT SHALLOW!
WHAT?
ARE YOU CHICKEN?

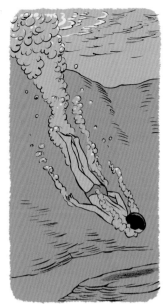

WHAK

I STILL HAVE A SCAR FROM CHILDHOOD...

SKRITCH SKRITCH

AH... SO YOU'RE REMEMBERING THINGS?

NO... JUST THAT.

JUST A SOLITARY BUBBLE RISING TO THE SURFACE.

PLUS, LOGICALLY, WE SHOULD BE IN THE MIDDLE OF A LUSH JUNGLE! WHERE'D ALL THAT LIFE GO?

HMM... I'D LIKE TO KNOW, TOO. BUT I MUST CONFESS THERE ARE LARGE GAPS IN MY RECENT RECORDS.

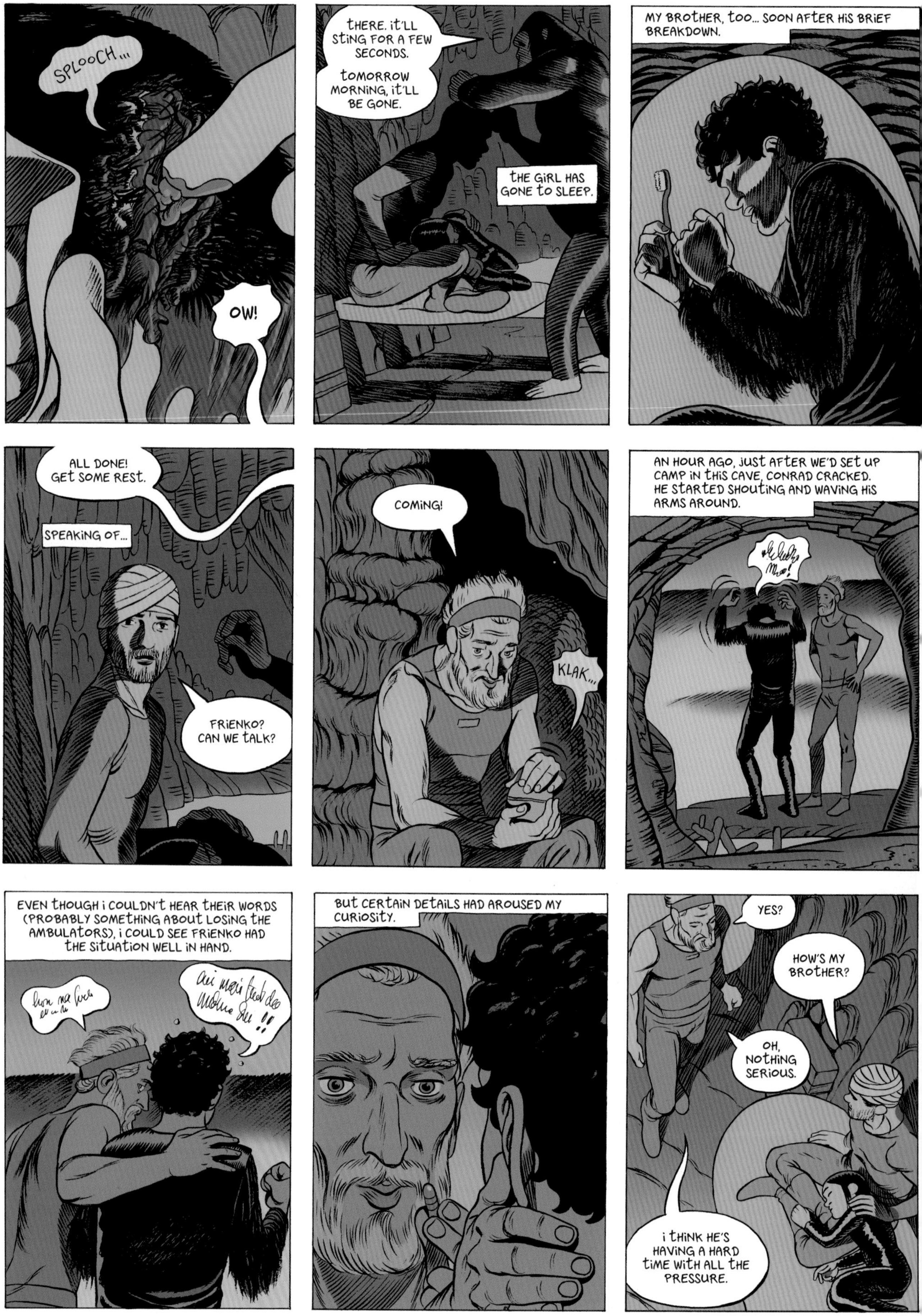
SPLOOCH...
OW!
THERE. IT'LL STING FOR A FEW SECONDS.
TOMORROW MORNING, IT'LL BE GONE.
THE GIRL HAS GONE TO SLEEP.
MY BROTHER, TOO... SOON AFTER HIS BRIEF BREAKDOWN.
ALL DONE! GET SOME REST.
SPEAKING OF...
FRIENKO? CAN WE TALK?
COMING!
KLAK...
AN HOUR AGO, JUST AFTER WE'D SET UP CAMP IN THIS CAVE, CONRAD CRACKED. HE STARTED SHOUTING AND WAVING HIS ARMS AROUND.
EVEN THOUGH I COULDN'T HEAR THEIR WORDS (PROBABLY SOMETHING ABOUT LOSING THE AMBULATORS), I COULD SEE FRIENKO HAD THE SITUATION WELL IN HAND.
BUT CERTAIN DETAILS HAD AROUSED MY CURIOSITY.
YES?
HOW'S MY BROTHER?
OH, NOTHING SERIOUS.
I THINK HE'S HAVING A HARD TIME WITH ALL THE PRESSURE.

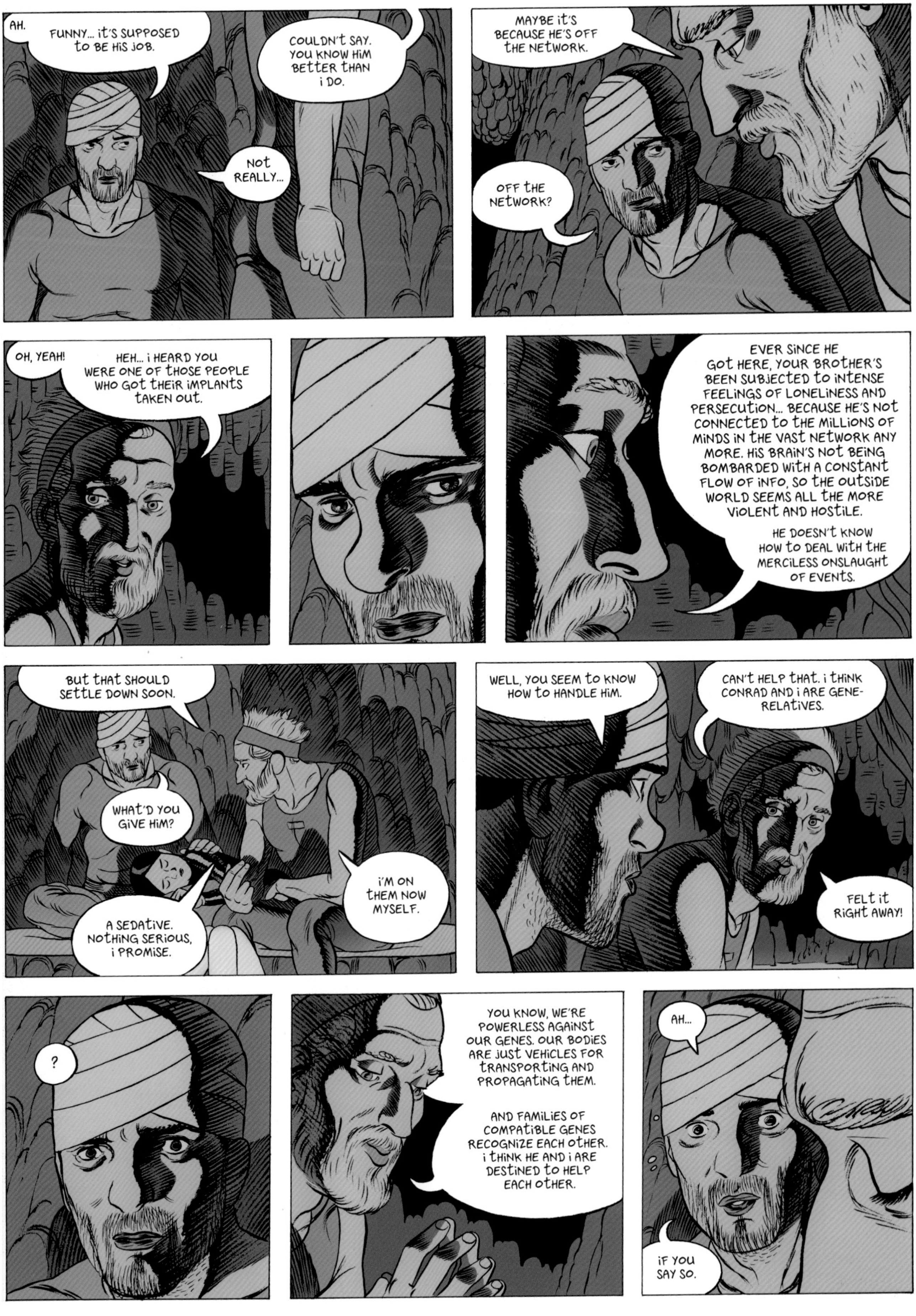
AH.
FUNNY... it'S SUPPOSED to BE HiS JOB.
COULDN'T SAY. YOU KNOW HiM BETTER THAN i DO.
Not REALLY...
MAYBE it'S BECAUSE HE'S OFF tHE NETWORK.
OFF tHE NETWORK?
OH, YEAH!
HEH... i HEARD YOU WERE ONE OF tHOSE PEOPLE WHO GOt tHEiR iMPLANtS tAKEN OUt.
EVER SiNCE HE GOt HERE, YOUR BROtHER'S BEEN SUBJECtED tO iNtENSE FEELiNGS OF LONELiNESS AND PERSECUtiON... BECAUSE HE'S NOt CONNECtED tO tHE MiLLiONS OF MiNDS iN tHE VASt NEtWORK ANY MORE. HiS BRAiN'S NOt BEiNG BOMBARDED WitH A CONStANt FLOW OF iNFO, SO tHE OUtSiDE WORLD SEEMS ALL tHE MORE ViOLENt AND HOStiLE.
HE DOESN't KNOW HOW tO DEAL WitH tHE MERCiLESS ONSLAUGHt OF EVENtS.
BUt tHAt SHOULD SEttLE DOWN SOON.
WHAt'D YOU GiVE HiM?
A SEDAtiVE. NOtHiNG SERiOUS, i PROMiSE.
i'M ON tHEM NOW MYSELF.
WELL, YOU SEEM tO KNOW HOW tO HANDLE HiM.
CAN't HELP tHAt. i tHiNK CONRAD AND i ARE GENE-RELAtiVES.
FELt it RiGHt AWAY!
?
YOU KNOW, WE'RE POWERLESS AGAiNSt OUR GENES. OUR BODiES ARE JUSt VEHiCLES FOR tRANSPORtiNG AND PROPAGAtiNG tHEM.
AND FAMiLiES OF COMPAtiBLE GENES RECOGNiZE EACH OtHER. i tHiNK HE AND i ARE DEStiNED tO HELP EACH OtHER.
AH...
iF YOU SAY SO.

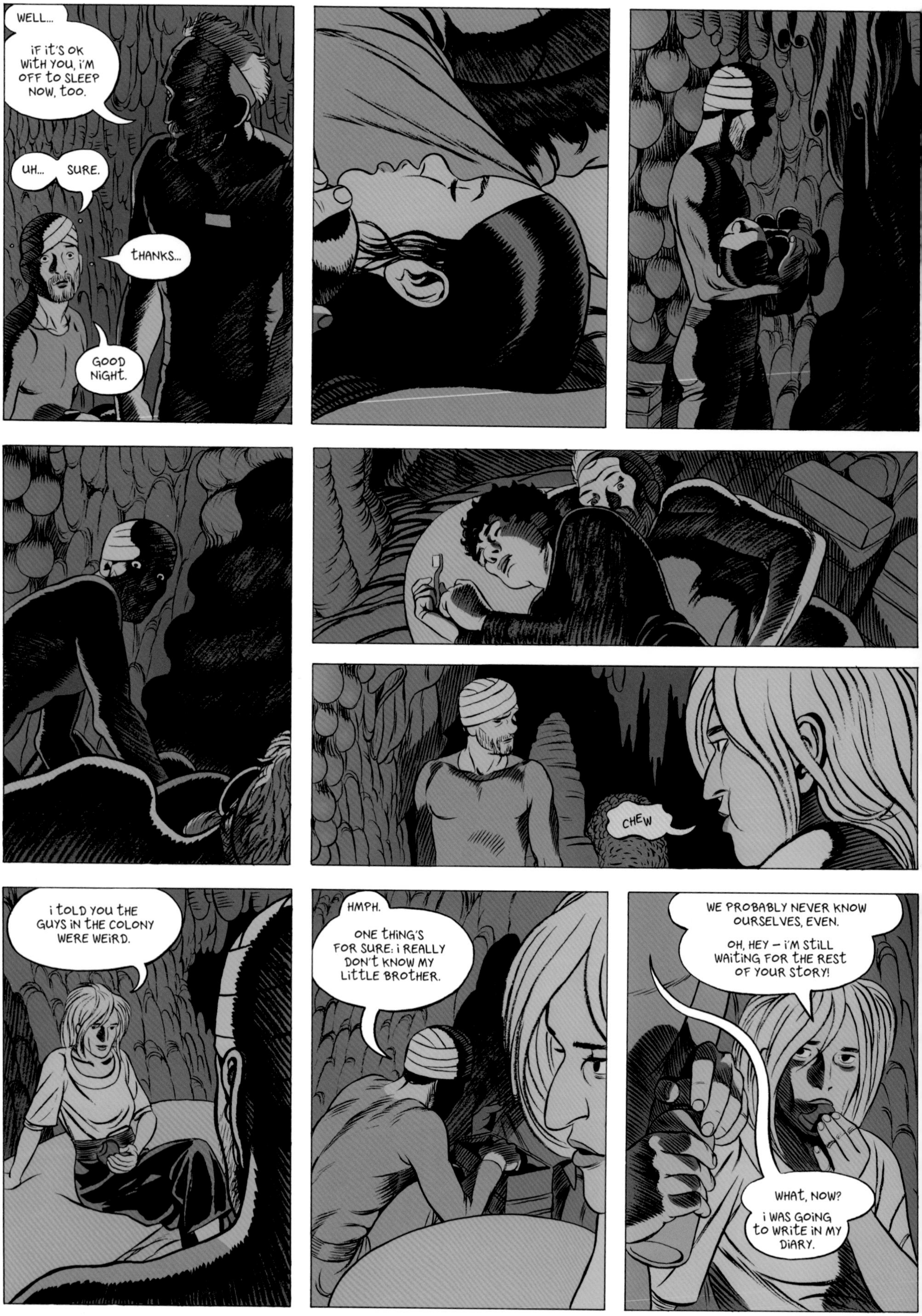

WELL...
iF iT'S OK WiTH YOU, i'M OFF TO SLEEP NOW, TOO.
UH...
SURE.
THANKS...
GOOD NiGHT.
CHEW
i TOLD YOU THE GUYS iN THE COLONY WERE WEiRD.
HMPH.
ONE THiNG'S FOR SURE: i REALLY DON'T KNOW MY LiTTLE BROTHER.
WE PROBABLY NEVER KNOW OURSELVES, EVEN.
OH, HEY – i'M STiLL WAiTiNG FOR THE REST OF YOUR STORY!
WHAT, NOW?
i WAS GOiNG TO WRiTE iN MY DiARY.

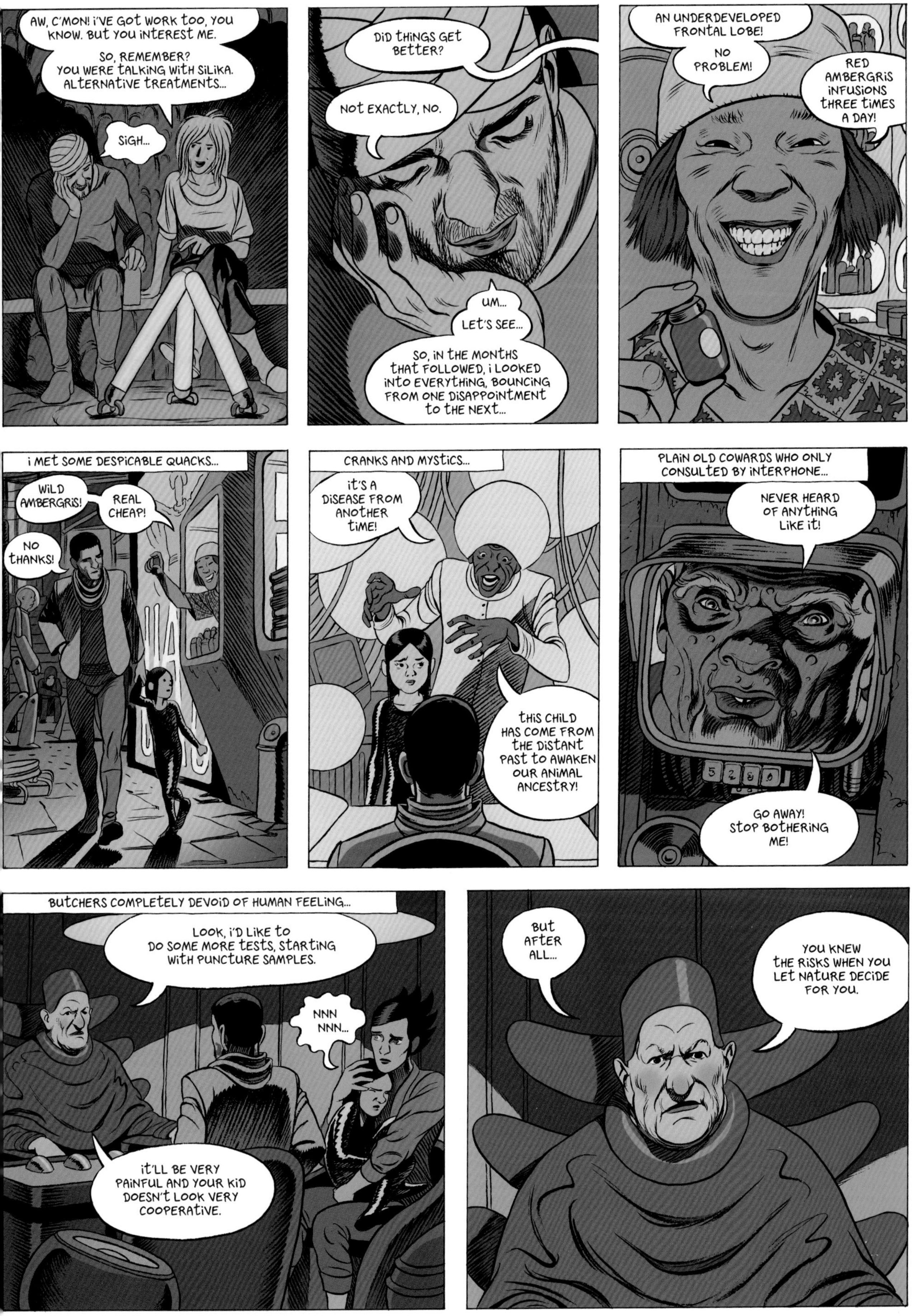
AW, C'MON! I'VE GOT WORK TOO, YOU KNOW. BUT YOU INTEREST ME.
SO, REMEMBER? YOU WERE TALKING WITH SILIKA. ALTERNATIVE TREATMENTS...
SIGH...
DID THINGS GET BETTER?
NOT EXACTLY, NO.
UM...
LET'S SEE...
SO, IN THE MONTHS THAT FOLLOWED, I LOOKED INTO EVERYTHING, BOUNCING FROM ONE DISAPPOINTMENT TO THE NEXT...
AN UNDERDEVELOPED FRONTAL LOBE!
NO PROBLEM!
RED AMBERGRIS INFUSIONS THREE TIMES A DAY!
I MET SOME DESPICABLE QUACKS...
WILD AMBERGRIS!
REAL CHEAP!
NO THANKS!
CRANKS AND MYSTICS...
IT'S A DISEASE FROM ANOTHER TIME!
THIS CHILD HAS COME FROM THE DISTANT PAST TO AWAKEN OUR ANIMAL ANCESTRY!
PLAIN OLD COWARDS WHO ONLY CONSULTED BY INTERPHONE...
NEVER HEARD OF ANYTHING LIKE IT!
GO AWAY! STOP BOTHERING ME!
BUTCHERS COMPLETELY DEVOID OF HUMAN FEELING...
LOOK, I'D LIKE TO DO SOME MORE TESTS, STARTING WITH PUNCTURE SAMPLES.
NNN NNN...
IT'LL BE VERY PAINFUL AND YOUR KID DOESN'T LOOK VERY COOPERATIVE.
BUT AFTER ALL...
YOU KNEW THE RISKS WHEN YOU LET NATURE DECIDE FOR YOU.

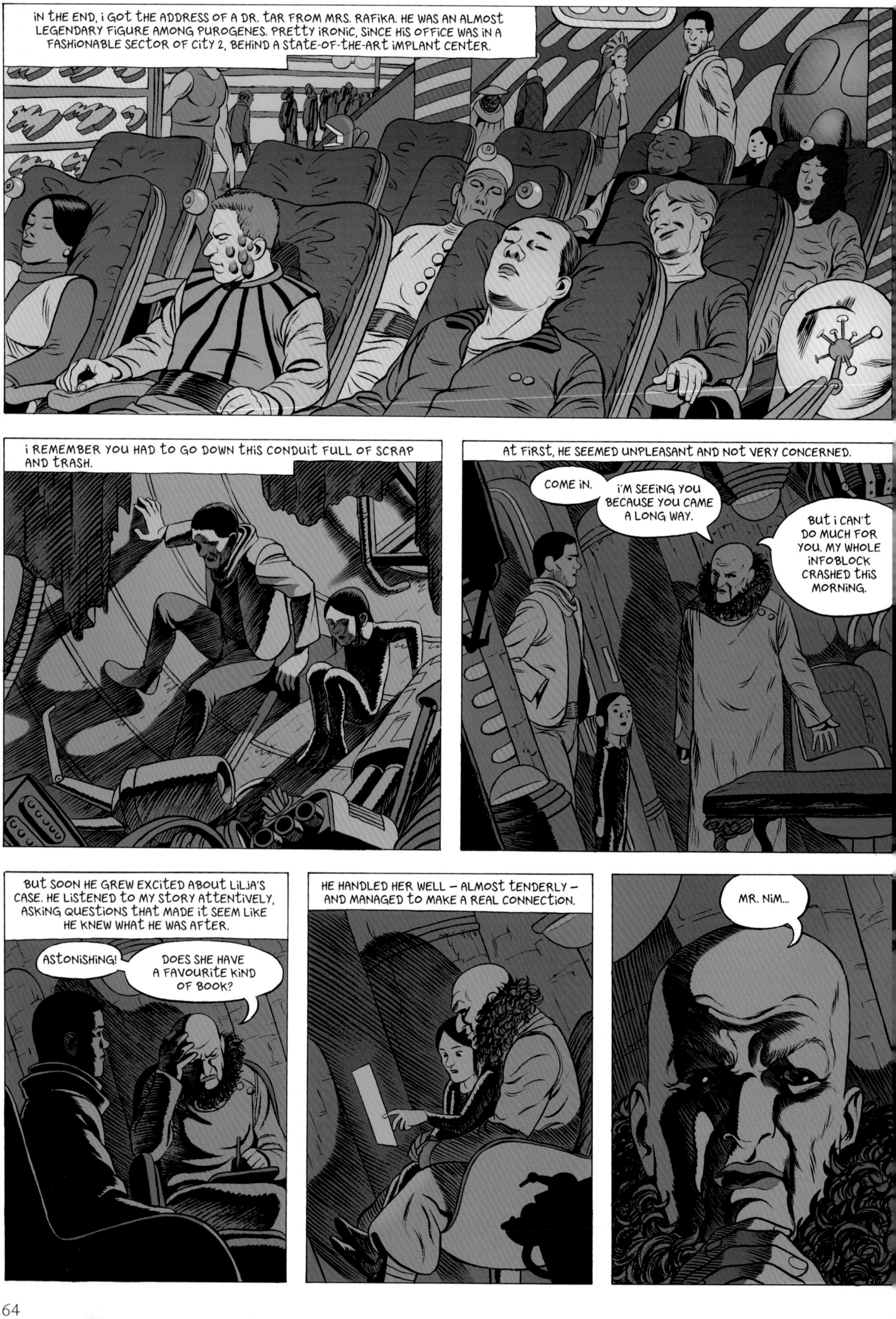

IN THE END, I GOT THE ADDRESS OF A DR. TAR FROM MRS. RAFIKA. HE WAS AN ALMOST LEGENDARY FIGURE AMONG PUROGENES. PRETTY IRONIC, SINCE HIS OFFICE WAS IN A FASHIONABLE SECTOR OF CITY 2, BEHIND A STATE-OF-THE-ART IMPLANT CENTER.
I REMEMBER YOU HAD TO GO DOWN THIS CONDUIT FULL OF SCRAP AND TRASH.
AT FIRST, HE SEEMED UNPLEASANT AND NOT VERY CONCERNED.
COME IN.
I'M SEEING YOU BECAUSE YOU CAME A LONG WAY.
BUT I CAN'T DO MUCH FOR YOU. MY WHOLE INFOBLOCK CRASHED THIS MORNING.
BUT SOON HE GREW EXCITED ABOUT LILJA'S CASE. HE LISTENED TO MY STORY ATTENTIVELY, ASKING QUESTIONS THAT MADE IT SEEM LIKE HE KNEW WHAT HE WAS AFTER.
ASTONISHING!
DOES SHE HAVE A FAVOURITE KIND OF BOOK?
HE HANDLED HER WELL – ALMOST TENDERLY – AND MANAGED TO MAKE A REAL CONNECTION.
MR. NIM...

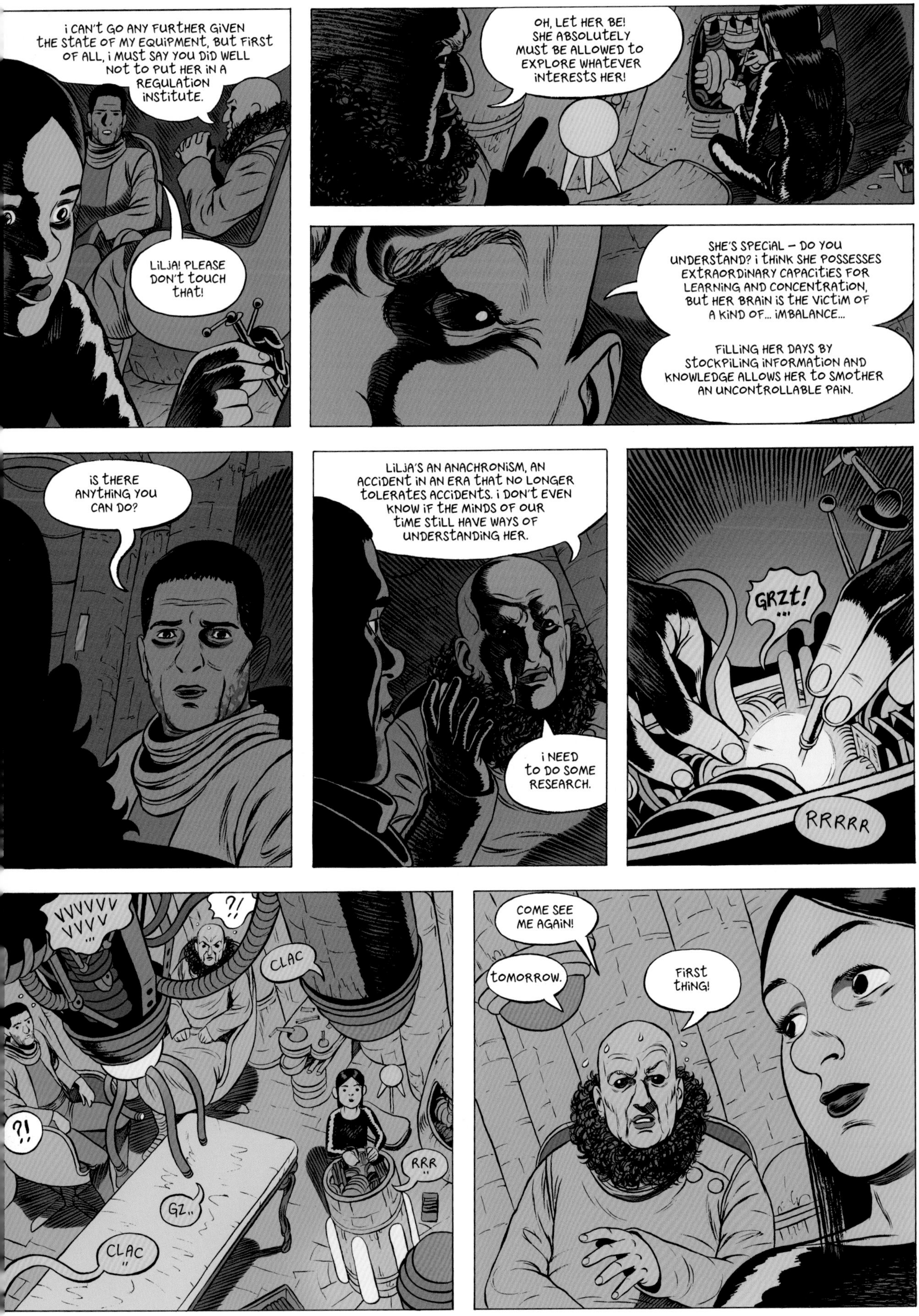

I CAN'T GO ANY FURTHER GIVEN THE STATE OF MY EQUIPMENT, BUT FIRST OF ALL, I MUST SAY YOU DID WELL NOT TO PUT HER IN A REGULATION INSTITUTE.
LILJA! PLEASE DON'T TOUCH THAT!
OH, LET HER BE! SHE ABSOLUTELY MUST BE ALLOWED TO EXPLORE WHATEVER INTERESTS HER!
SHE'S SPECIAL – DO YOU UNDERSTAND? I THINK SHE POSSESSES EXTRAORDINARY CAPACITIES FOR LEARNING AND CONCENTRATION, BUT HER BRAIN IS THE VICTIM OF A KIND OF... IMBALANCE...
FILLING HER DAYS BY STOCKPILING INFORMATION AND KNOWLEDGE ALLOWS HER TO SMOTHER AN UNCONTROLLABLE PAIN.
IS THERE ANYTHING YOU CAN DO?
LILJA'S AN ANACHRONISM, AN ACCIDENT IN AN ERA THAT NO LONGER TOLERATES ACCIDENTS. I DON'T EVEN KNOW IF THE MINDS OF OUR TIME STILL HAVE WAYS OF UNDERSTANDING HER.
I NEED TO DO SOME RESEARCH.
GRZT! ...
RRRRR
VVVVVV VVVV ...
?!
CLAC
?!
RRR ..
GZ..
CLAC ..
COME SEE ME AGAIN!
TOMORROW.
FIRST THING!

EVEN AS I WAS TAKING ALL THESE STEPS, SILIKA AND I WERE LOST IN A RELATIONSHIP LABYRINTH. THE WARM FOG OF ROUTINE, THE BUILD-UP OF ACERBIC DETAILS... THE PATTERNS THAT SET IN.

SHE WAS THE LEVEL-HEADED, STABLE ONE...

I WAS AN EASYGOING SLAVE TO PIPE DREAMS.

BIT BY BIT, I STARTED EXPLOITING MY POSITION, BECOMING SCORNFUL AND MANIPULATIVE.

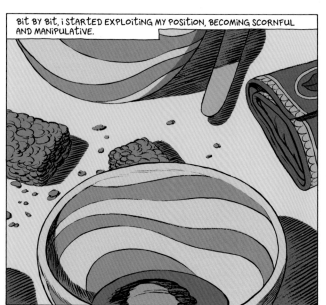

WHILE SILIKA SET HERSELF UP AS A SHE-WOLF, WARY FOR HER CUB.

I CAN STILL HEAR THE TONE OF HER VOICE WHEN I TOLD HER I'D MADE AN APPOINTMENT WITH DR. TAR.

YOU STILL BELIEVE IN HIM?

SUFFUSED WITH BITTERNESS AND PITY...

WE WERE SO WORN OUT AFTER OUR APPOINTMENT THAT HER BEHAVIOUR DIDN'T SEEM SUSPECT.

THIS TIME IT'S FOR REAL!

I TOLD YOU!

HE KNOWS WHAT HE'S TALKING ABOUT!

AND LILJA LIKES HIM!

SEE?

IF YOU JUST LISTENED TO ME MORE OFTEN...

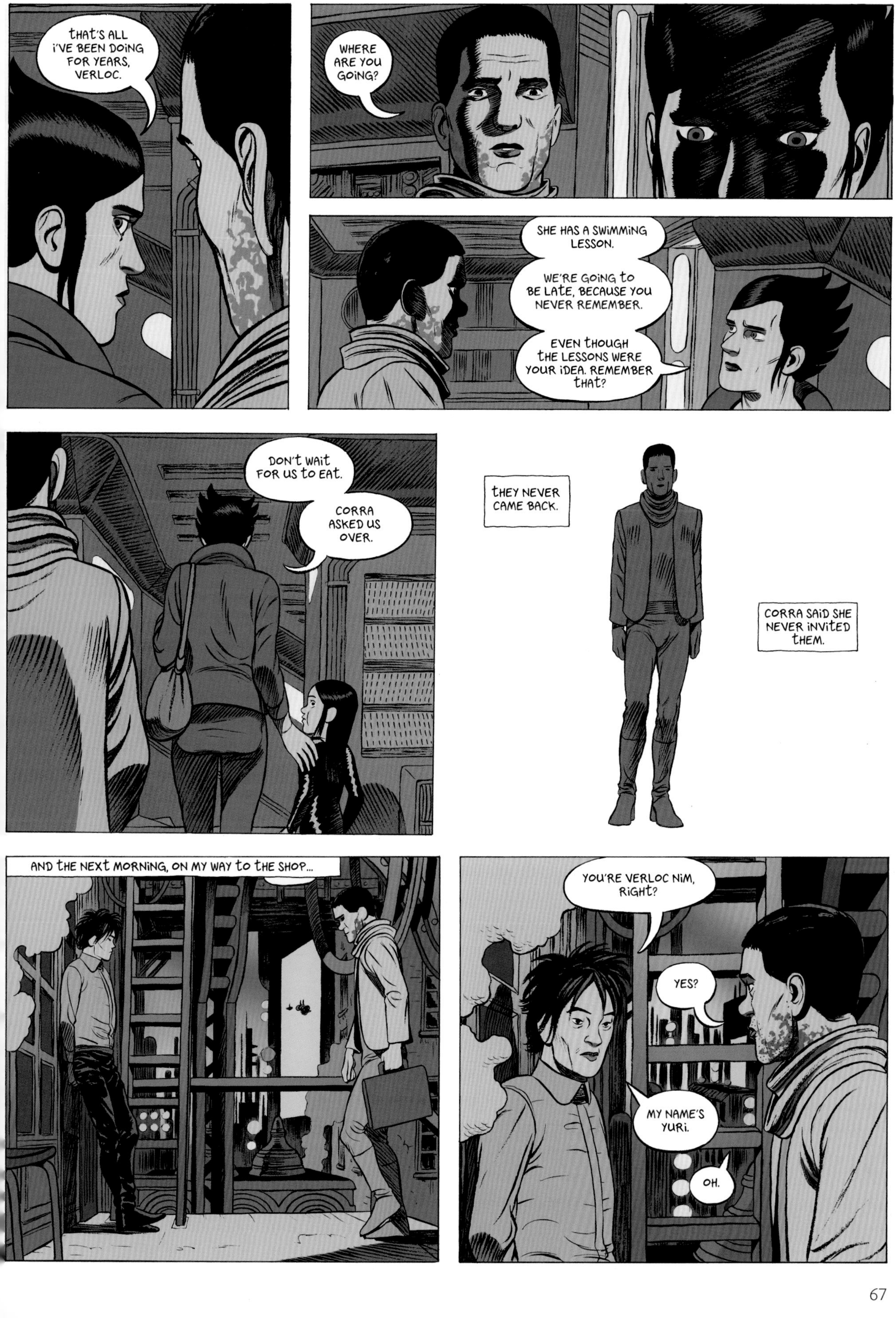
THAT'S ALL I'VE BEEN DOING FOR YEARS, VERLOC.
WHERE ARE YOU GOING?
SHE HAS A SWIMMING LESSON.
WE'RE GOING TO BE LATE, BECAUSE YOU NEVER REMEMBER.
EVEN THOUGH THE LESSONS WERE YOUR IDEA. REMEMBER THAT?
DON'T WAIT FOR US TO EAT.
CORRA ASKED US OVER.
THEY NEVER CAME BACK.
CORRA SAID SHE NEVER INVITED THEM.
AND THE NEXT MORNING, ON MY WAY TO THE SHOP...
YOU'RE VERLOC NIM, RIGHT?
YES?
MY NAME'S YURI.
OH.

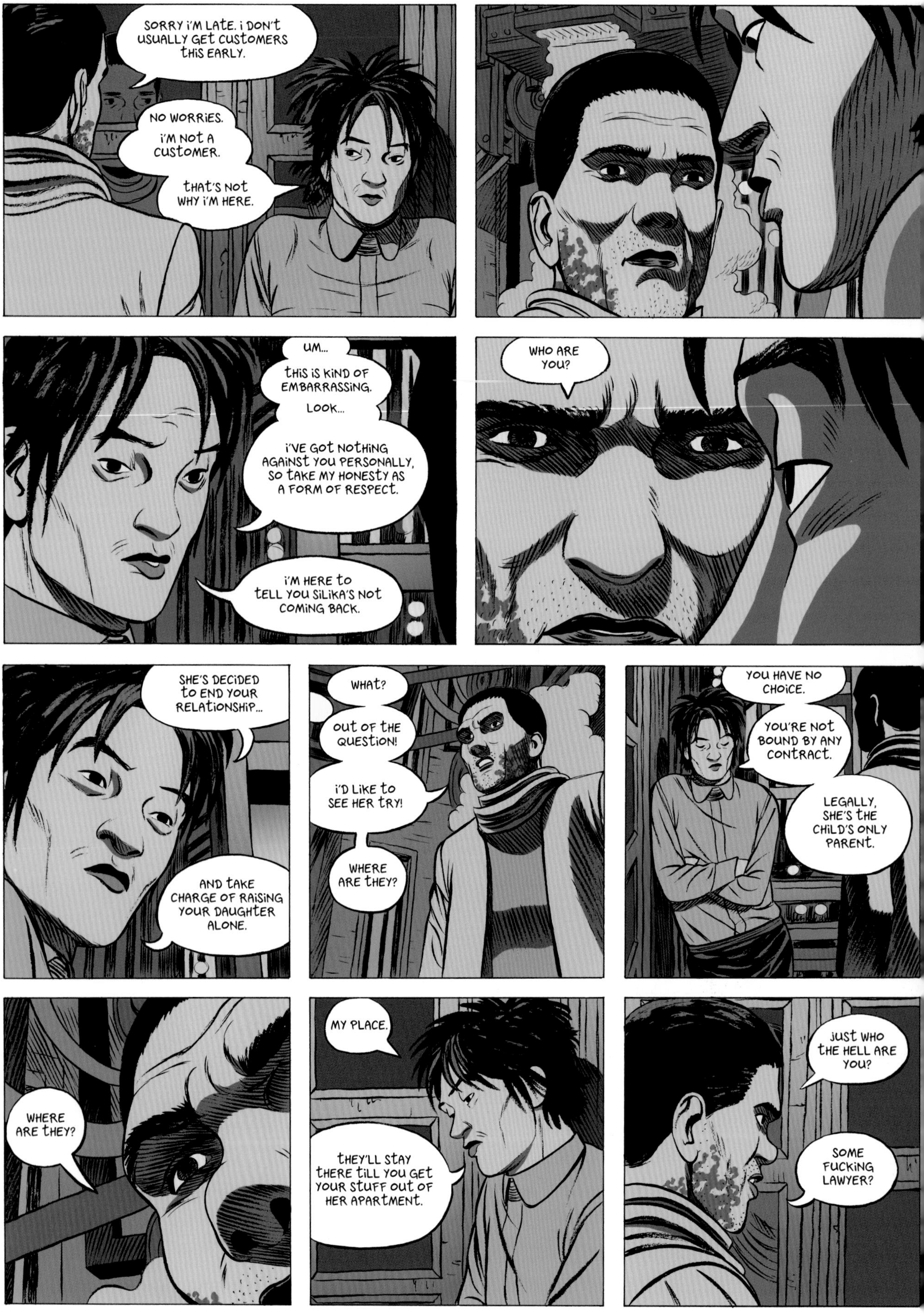
SORRY I'M LATE. I DON'T USUALLY GET CUSTOMERS THIS EARLY.
NO WORRIES.
I'M NOT A CUSTOMER.
THAT'S NOT WHY I'M HERE.
UM...
THIS IS KIND OF EMBARRASSING.
LOOK...
I'VE GOT NOTHING AGAINST YOU PERSONALLY, SO TAKE MY HONESTY AS A FORM OF RESPECT.
I'M HERE TO TELL YOU SILIKA'S NOT COMING BACK.
WHO ARE YOU?
SHE'S DECIDED TO END YOUR RELATIONSHIP...
AND TAKE CHARGE OF RAISING YOUR DAUGHTER ALONE.
WHAT?
OUT OF THE QUESTION!
I'D LIKE TO SEE HER TRY!
WHERE ARE THEY?
YOU HAVE NO CHOICE.
YOU'RE NOT BOUND BY ANY CONTRACT.
LEGALLY, SHE'S THE CHILD'S ONLY PARENT.
WHERE ARE THEY?
MY PLACE.
THEY'LL STAY THERE TILL YOU GET YOUR STUFF OUT OF HER APARTMENT.
JUST WHO THE HELL ARE YOU?
SOME FUCKING LAWYER?

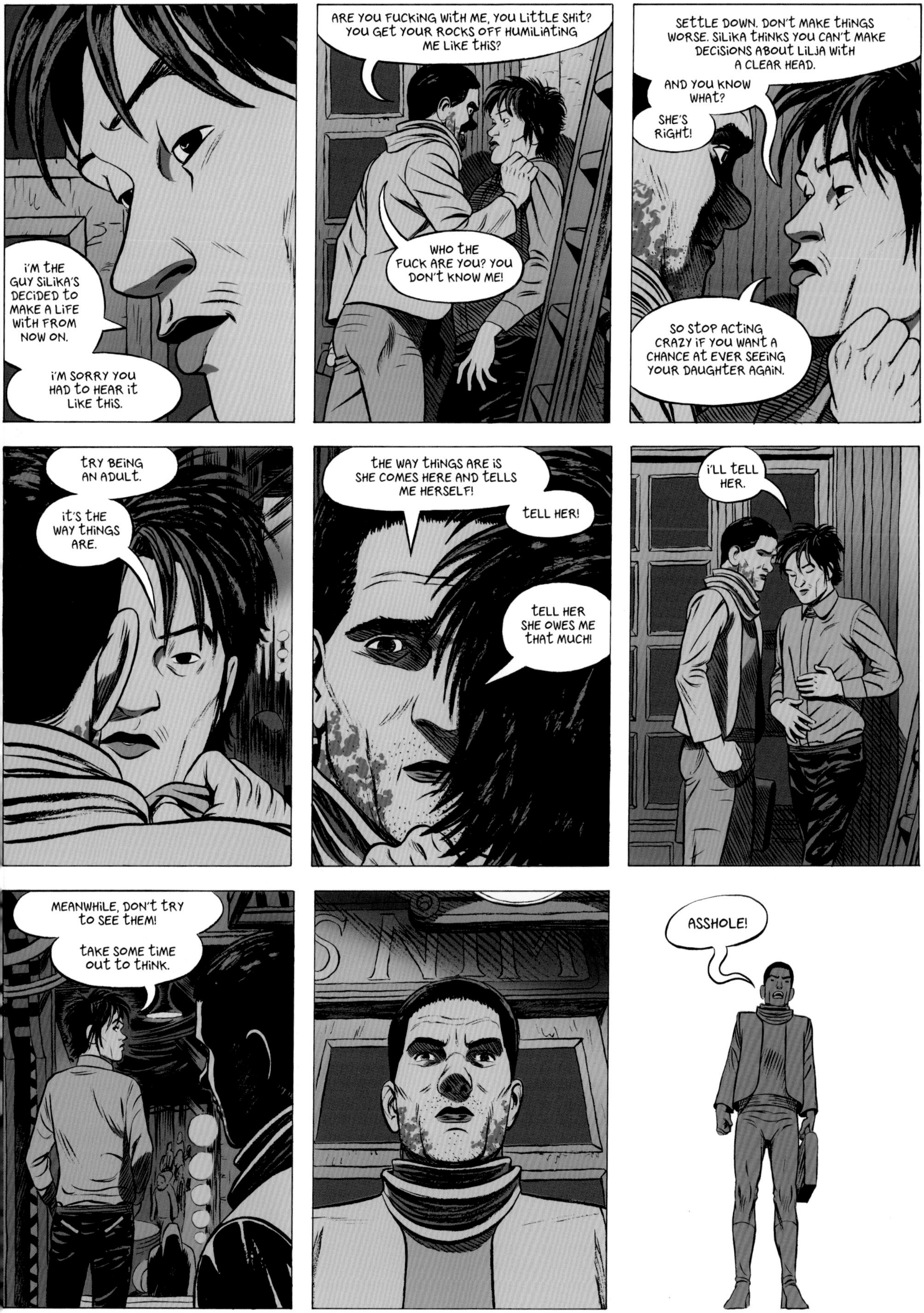
I'M THE GUY SILIKA'S DECIDED TO MAKE A LIFE WITH FROM NOW ON.
I'M SORRY YOU HAD TO HEAR IT LIKE THIS.
ARE YOU FUCKING WITH ME, YOU LITTLE SHIT? YOU GET YOUR ROCKS OFF HUMILIATING ME LIKE THIS?
WHO THE FUCK ARE YOU? YOU DON'T KNOW ME!
SETTLE DOWN. DON'T MAKE THINGS WORSE. SILIKA THINKS YOU CAN'T MAKE DECISIONS ABOUT LILJA WITH A CLEAR HEAD.
AND YOU KNOW WHAT?
SHE'S RIGHT!
SO STOP ACTING CRAZY IF YOU WANT A CHANCE AT EVER SEEING YOUR DAUGHTER AGAIN.
TRY BEING AN ADULT.
IT'S THE WAY THINGS ARE.
THE WAY THINGS ARE IS SHE COMES HERE AND TELLS ME HERSELF!
TELL HER!
TELL HER SHE OWES ME THAT MUCH!
I'LL TELL HER.
MEANWHILE, DON'T TRY TO SEE THEM!
TAKE SOME TIME OUT TO THINK.
ASSHOLE!

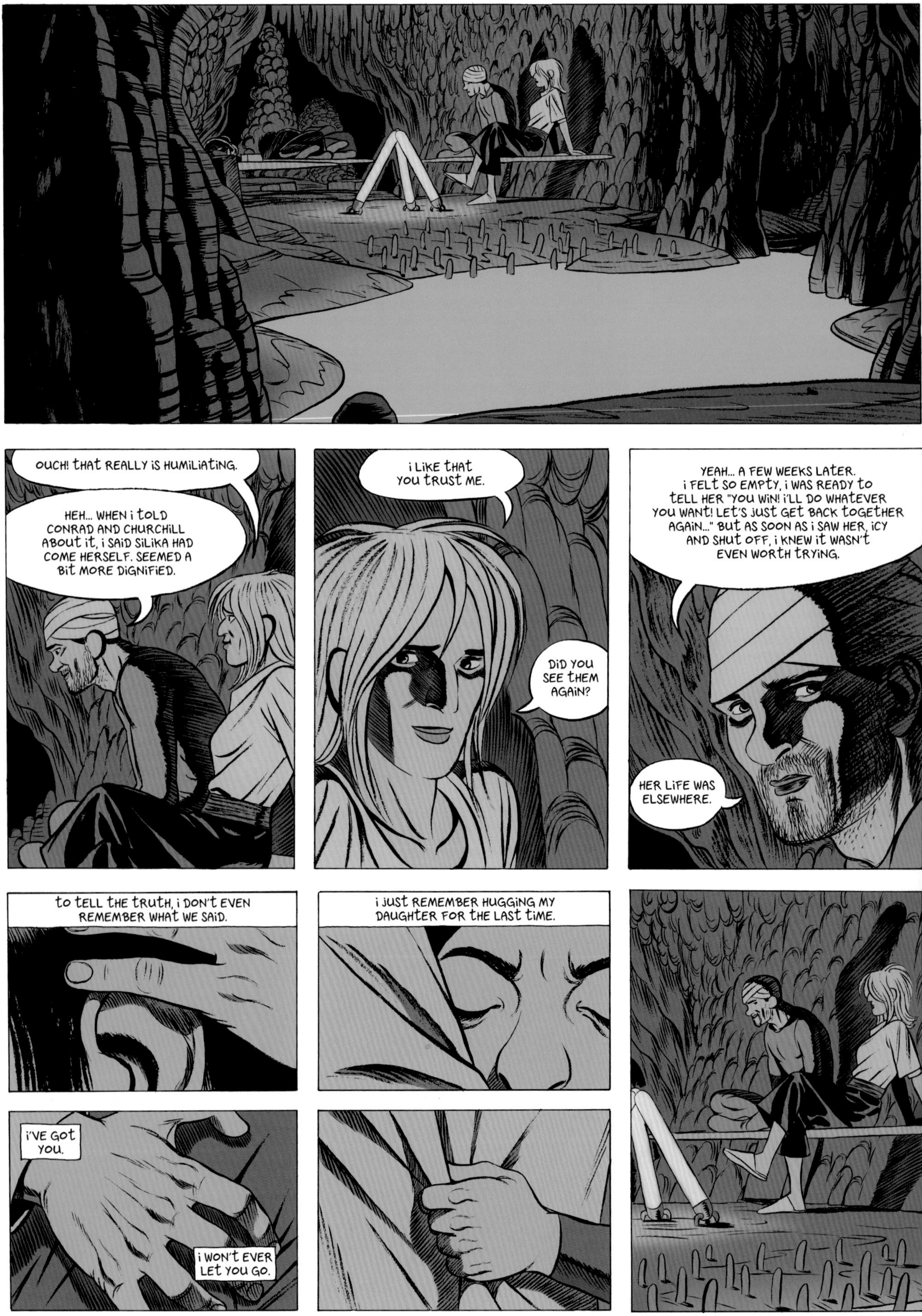
OUCH! THAT REALLY IS HUMILIATING.
HEH... WHEN I TOLD CONRAD AND CHURCHILL ABOUT IT, I SAID SILIKA HAD COME HERSELF. SEEMED A BIT MORE DIGNIFIED.
I LIKE THAT YOU TRUST ME.
DID YOU SEE THEM AGAIN?
YEAH... A FEW WEEKS LATER. I FELT SO EMPTY, I WAS READY TO TELL HER "YOU WIN! I'LL DO WHATEVER YOU WANT! LET'S JUST GET BACK TOGETHER AGAIN..." BUT AS SOON AS I SAW HER, ICY AND SHUT OFF, I KNEW IT WASN'T EVEN WORTH TRYING.
HER LIFE WAS ELSEWHERE.
TO TELL THE TRUTH, I DON'T EVEN REMEMBER WHAT WE SAID.
I JUST REMEMBER HUGGING MY DAUGHTER FOR THE LAST TIME.
I'VE GOT YOU.
I WON'T EVER LET YOU GO.

I SAW HER TWICE MORE LIKE THAT, AND THEN ONE LAST TIME, WHEN I GOT BEATEN UP BY BODYGUARDS.

AAMA KNOWS YOUR DAUGHTER. THAT MUCH IS CLEAR.

THEY WERE BOTH BORN AT THE SAME TIME.

AS A RESULT, AAMA KNOWS YOU, TOO.

GOTTA GO WORK!

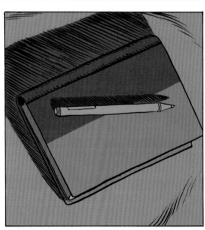

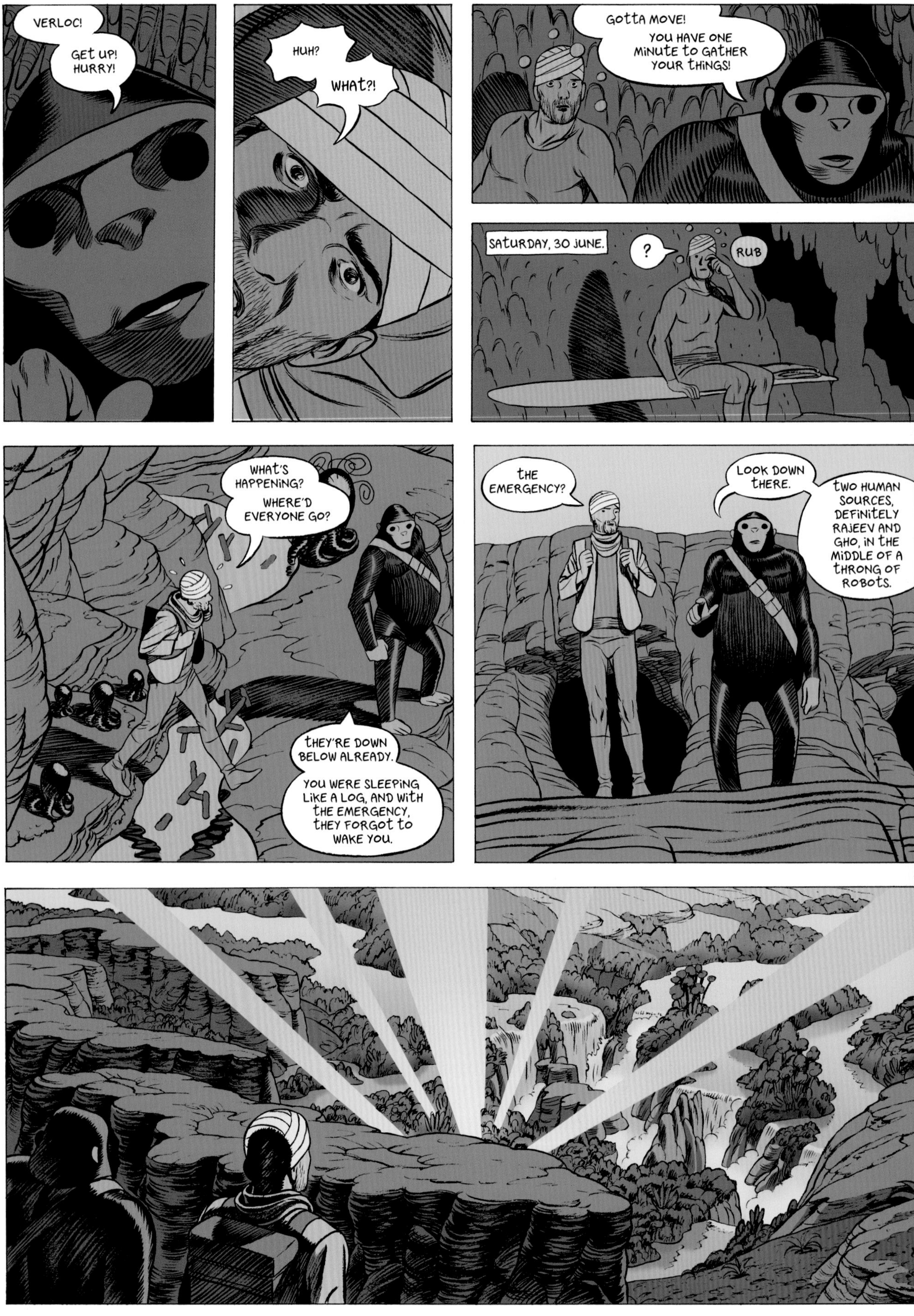
VERLOC!
GET UP! HURRY!
HUH?
WHAT?!
GOTTA MOVE!
YOU HAVE ONE MINUTE TO GATHER YOUR THINGS!
SATURDAY, 30 JUNE.
?
RUB
WHAT'S HAPPENING?
WHERE'D EVERYONE GO?
THEY'RE DOWN BELOW ALREADY.
YOU WERE SLEEPING LIKE A LOG, AND WITH THE EMERGENCY, THEY FORGOT TO WAKE YOU.
THE EMERGENCY?
LOOK DOWN THERE.
TWO HUMAN SOURCES, DEFINITELY RAJEEV AND GHO, IN THE MIDDLE OF A THRONG OF ROBOTS.

BEAUTIFUL...

MUCH LESS SO CLOSER UP.

YOU CAN TAKE OFF THAT BANDAGE.

HOW'D THEY GET DOWN?

UM...

HOW SHOULD I PUT IT? IN SHORT...

LIKE THIS!

AH!

AAAAAAAA

CHLOUF

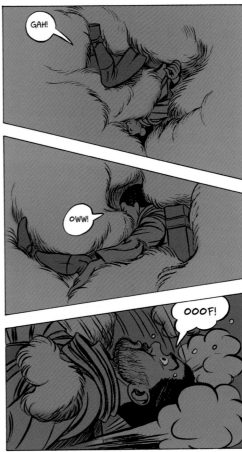

GAH!

OWW!

OOOF!

73

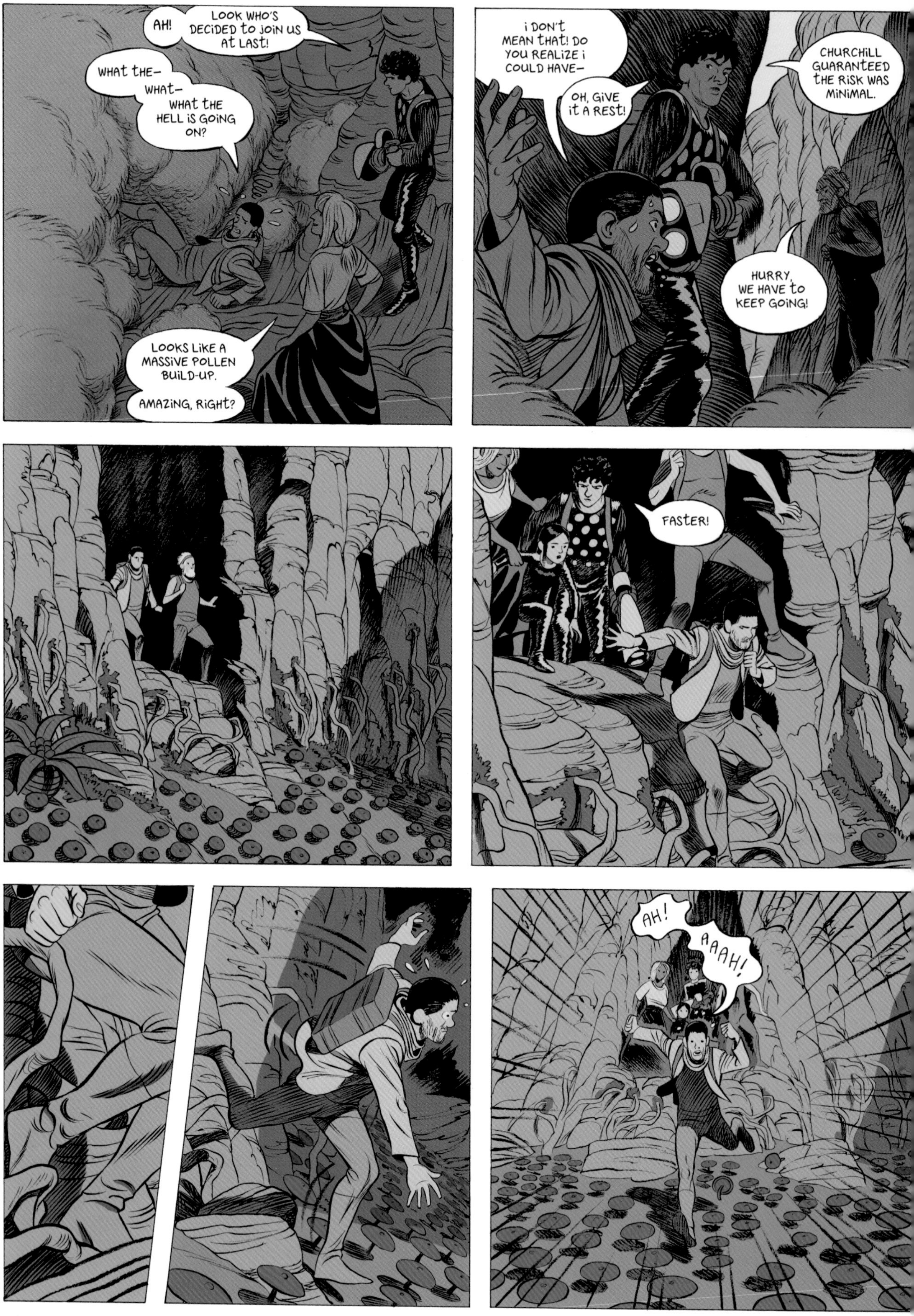
AH!
LOOK WHO'S DECIDED TO JOIN US AT LAST!
WHAT THE–
WHAT–
WHAT THE HELL IS GOING ON?
LOOKS LIKE A MASSIVE POLLEN BUILD-UP.
AMAZING, RIGHT?
I DON'T MEAN THAT! DO YOU REALIZE I COULD HAVE–
OH, GIVE IT A REST!
CHURCHILL GUARANTEED THE RISK WAS MINIMAL.
HURRY, WE HAVE TO KEEP GOING!
FASTER!
AH!
AAAH!

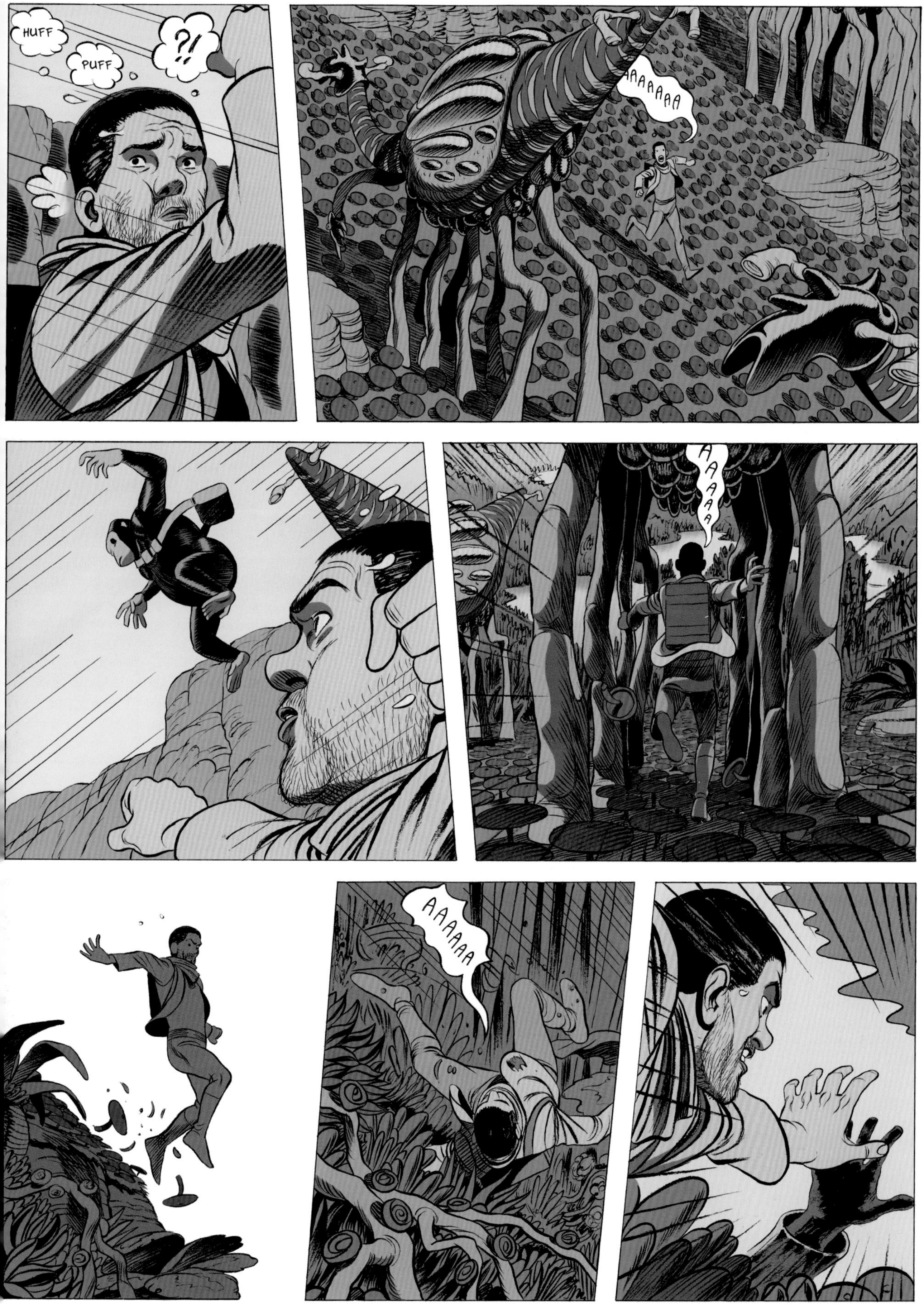
HUFF
PUFF
?!
AAAAAAA
AAAAA
AAAAAA

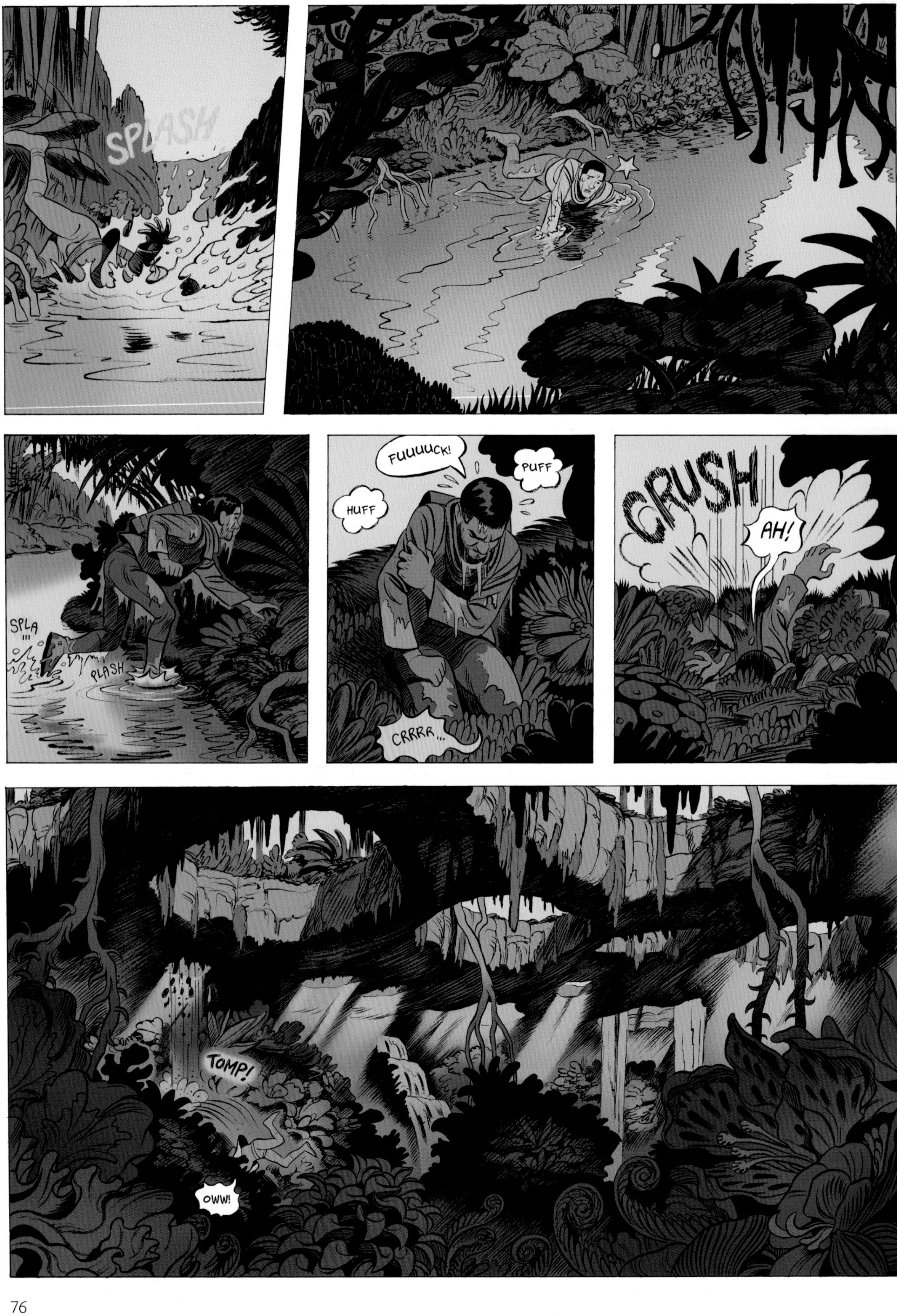
SPLASH
FUUUUCK!
HUFF
PUFF
SPLA
PLASH
CRRRR...
CRUSH
AH!
TOMP!
OWW!

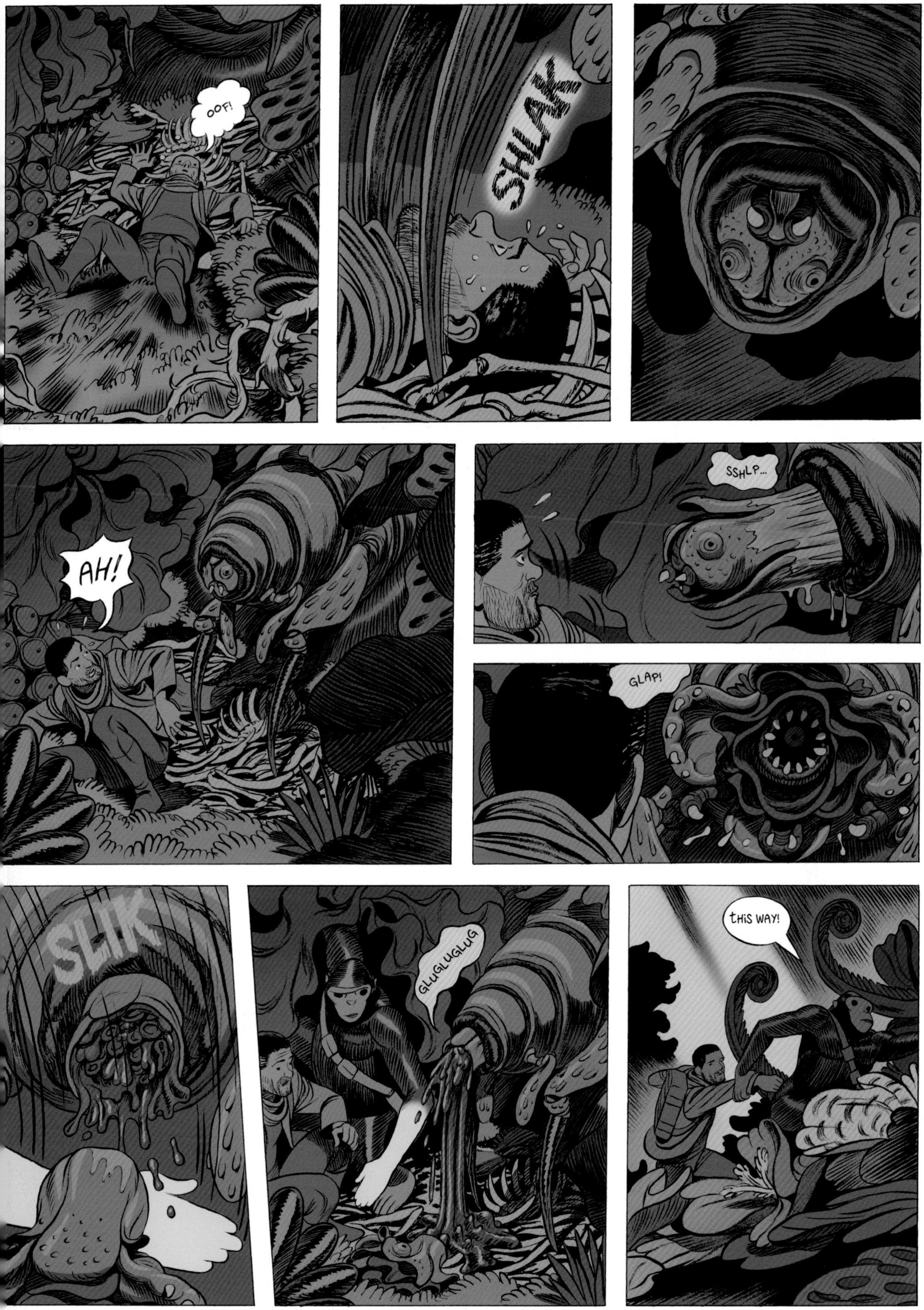
OOF!
SHLAK
AH!
SSHLP...
GLAP!
SLIK
GLUGLUGLUG
tHIS WAY!

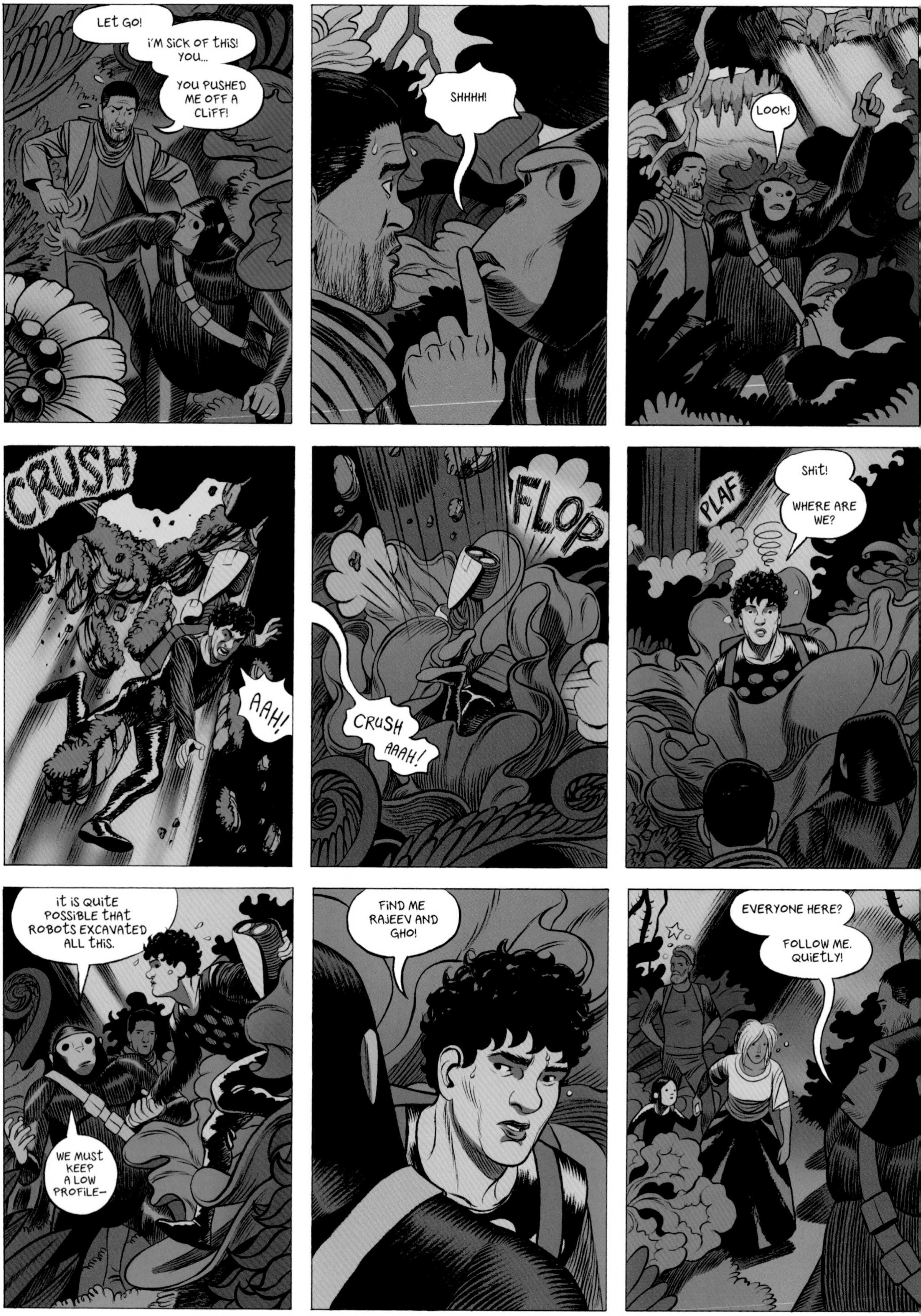
LET GO!
I'M SICK OF THIS! YOU...
YOU PUSHED ME OFF A CLIFF!
SHHHH!
LOOK!
CRUSH
AAH!
FLOP
CRUSH
AAAH!
PLAF
SHIT!
WHERE ARE WE?
IT IS QUITE POSSIBLE THAT ROBOTS EXCAVATED ALL THIS.
WE MUST KEEP A LOW PROFILE–
FIND ME RAJEEV AND GHO!
EVERYONE HERE?
FOLLOW ME. QUIETLY!

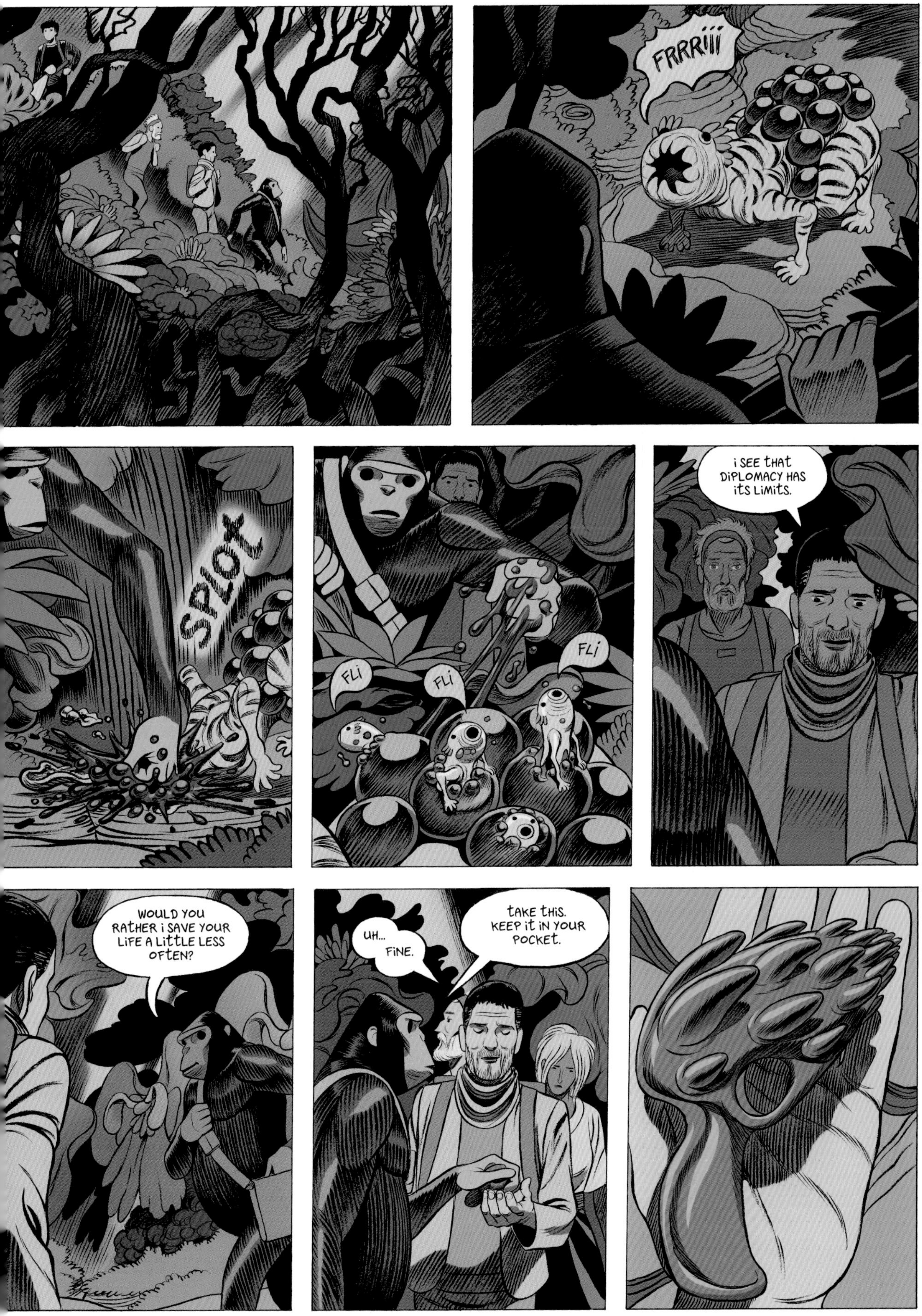
FRRRiii
SPLOX
FLi
FLi
FLi
i SEE tHAt DiPLOMACY HAS itS LiMitS.
WOULD YOU RATHER i SAVE YOUR LiFE A LittLE LESS OFtEN?
UH... FiNE.
tAKE tHiS. KEEP it iN YOUR POCKEt.

STOP!

GRENADE!

GET DOWN!

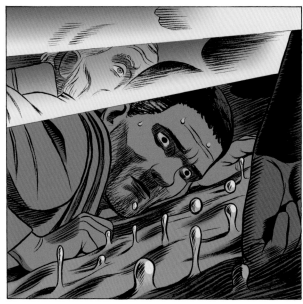

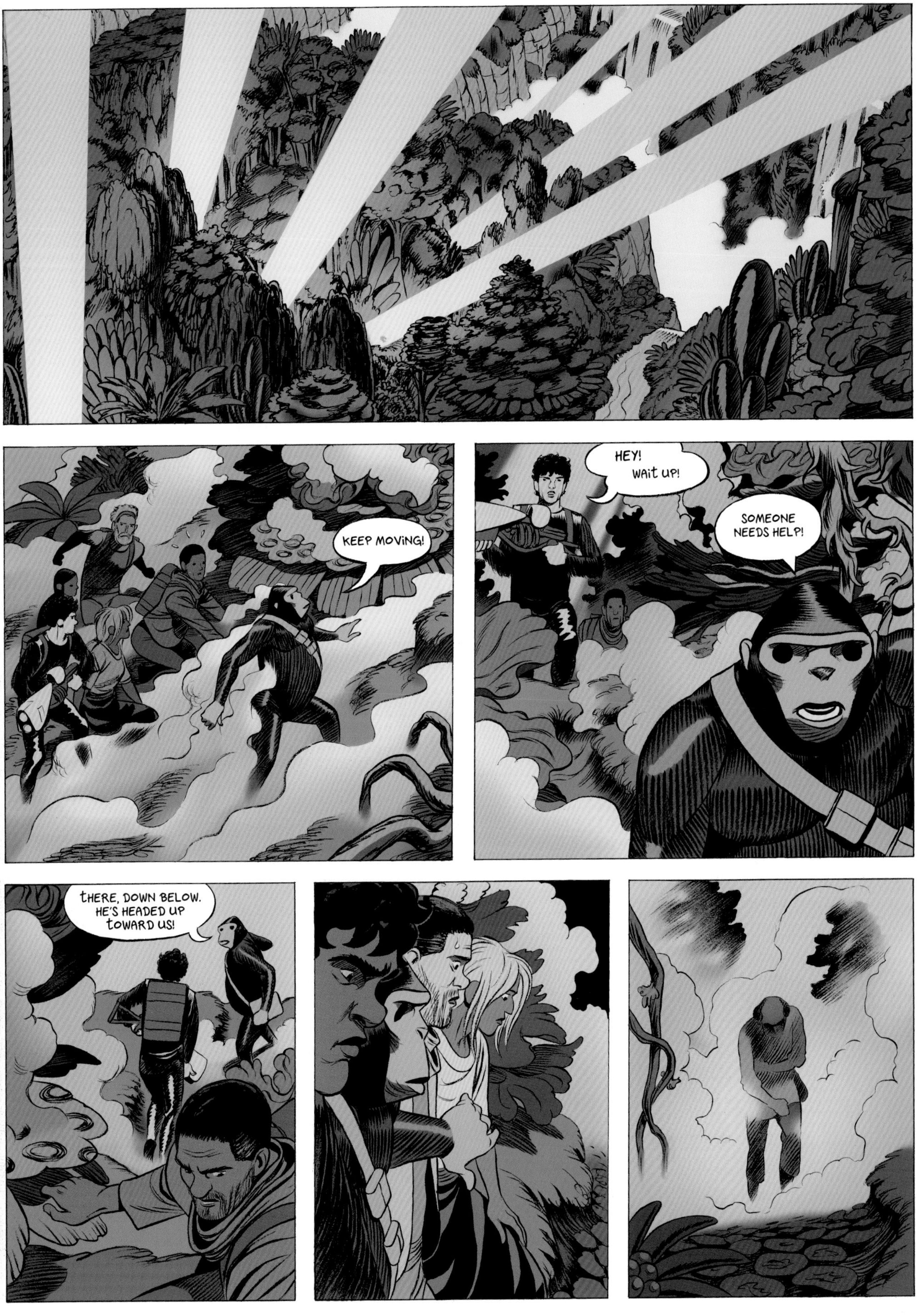
KEEP MOVING!
HEY! WAIT UP!
SOMEONE NEEDS HELP!
THERE, DOWN BELOW. HE'S HEADED UP TOWARD US!

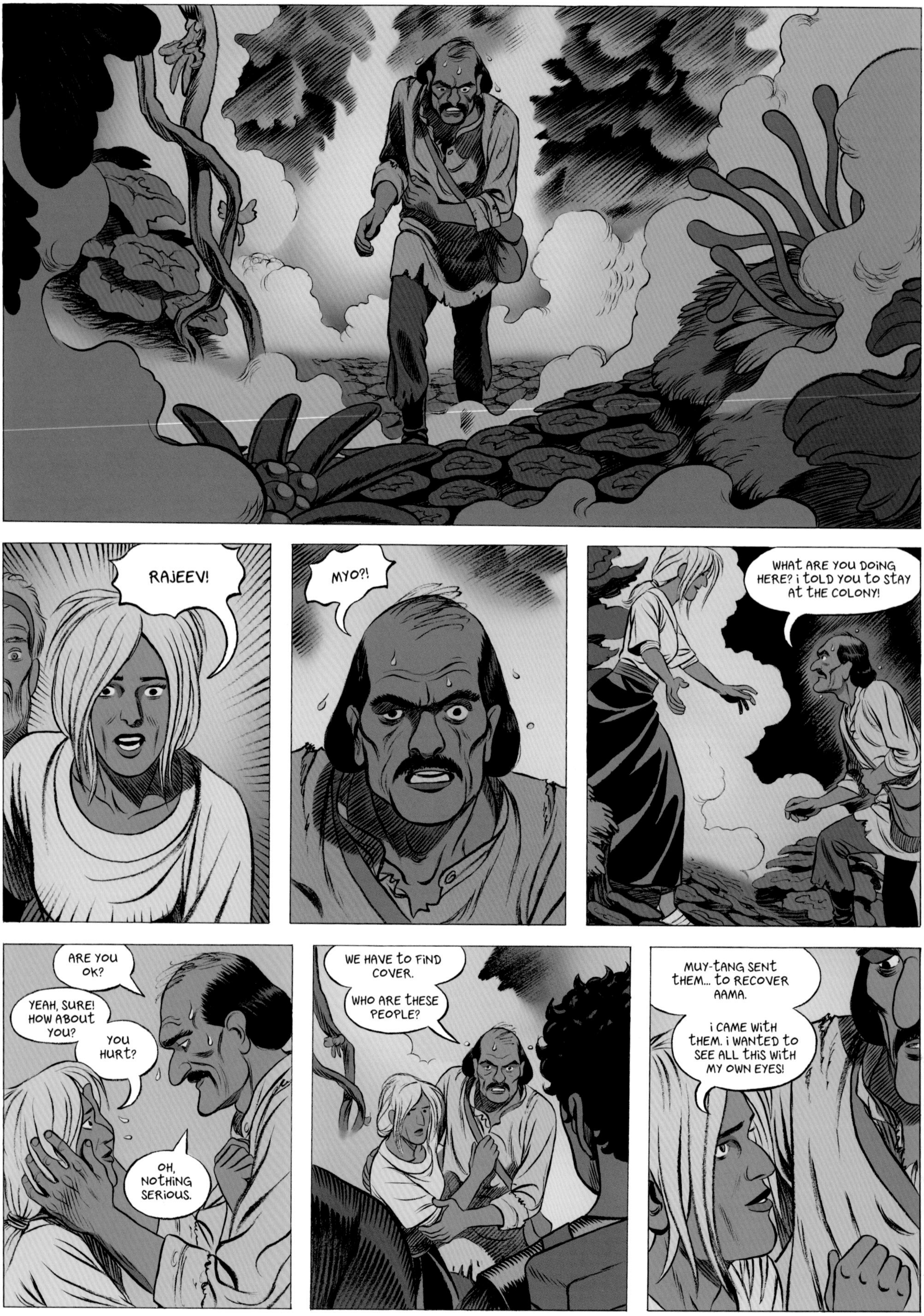
RAJEEV!
MYO?!
WHAT ARE YOU DOING HERE? I TOLD YOU TO STAY AT THE COLONY!
ARE YOU OK?
YEAH, SURE! HOW ABOUT YOU?
YOU HURT?
OH, NOTHING SERIOUS.
WE HAVE TO FIND COVER.
WHO ARE THESE PEOPLE?
MUY-TANG SENT THEM... TO RECOVER AAMA.
I CAME WITH THEM. I WANTED TO SEE ALL THIS WITH MY OWN EYES!

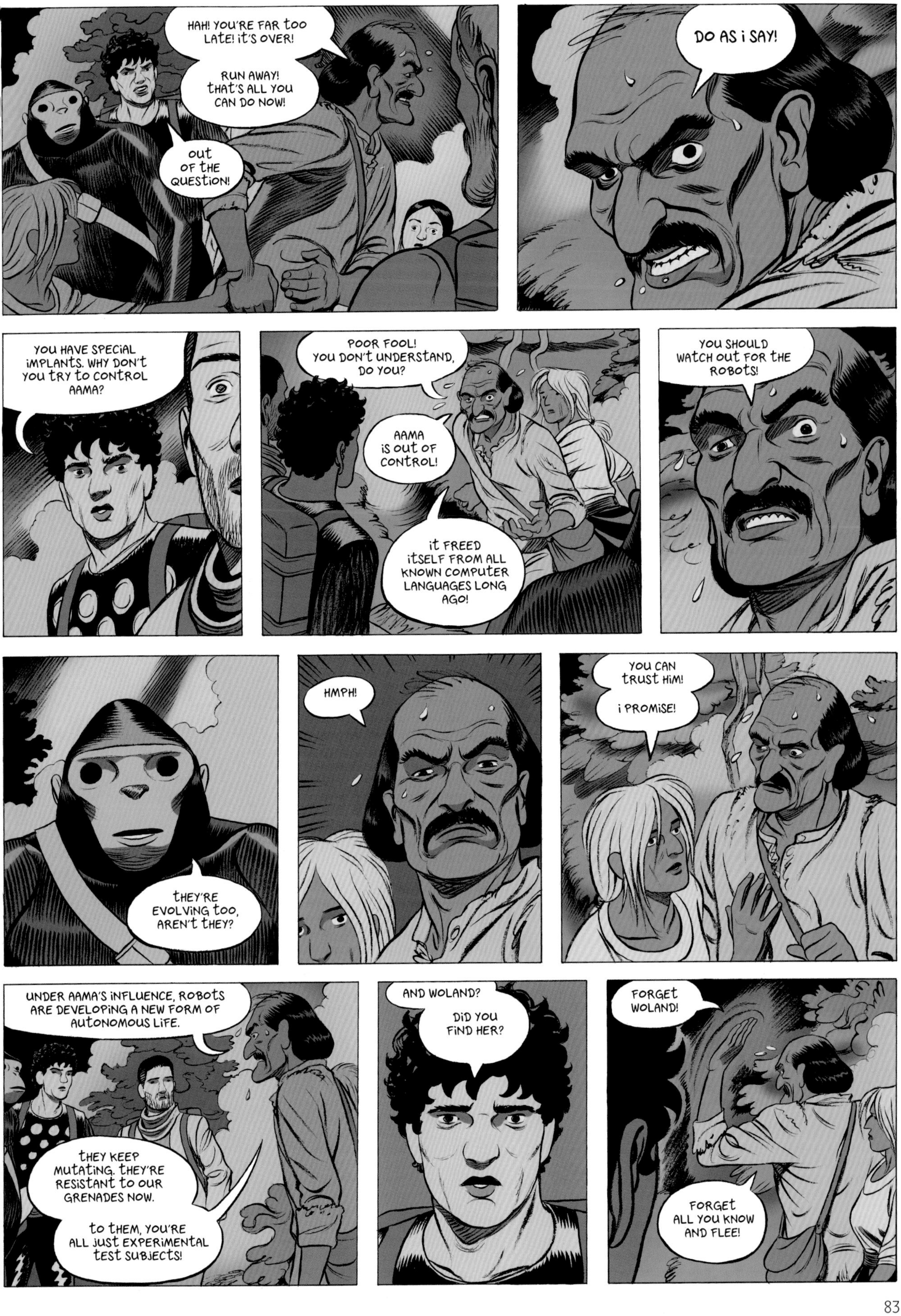
HAH! YOU'RE FAR TOO LATE! IT'S OVER!
RUN AWAY! THAT'S ALL YOU CAN DO NOW!
OUT OF THE QUESTION!
DO AS I SAY!
YOU HAVE SPECIAL IMPLANTS. WHY DON'T YOU TRY TO CONTROL AAMA?
POOR FOOL! YOU DON'T UNDERSTAND, DO YOU?
AAMA IS OUT OF CONTROL!
IT FREED ITSELF FROM ALL KNOWN COMPUTER LANGUAGES LONG AGO!
YOU SHOULD WATCH OUT FOR THE ROBOTS!
THEY'RE EVOLVING TOO, AREN'T THEY?
HMPH!
YOU CAN TRUST HIM!
I PROMISE!
UNDER AAMA'S INFLUENCE, ROBOTS ARE DEVELOPING A NEW FORM OF AUTONOMOUS LIFE.
THEY KEEP MUTATING. THEY'RE RESISTANT TO OUR GRENADES NOW.
TO THEM, YOU'RE ALL JUST EXPERIMENTAL TEST SUBJECTS!
AND WOLAND?
DID YOU FIND HER?
FORGET WOLAND!
FORGET ALL YOU KNOW AND FLEE!

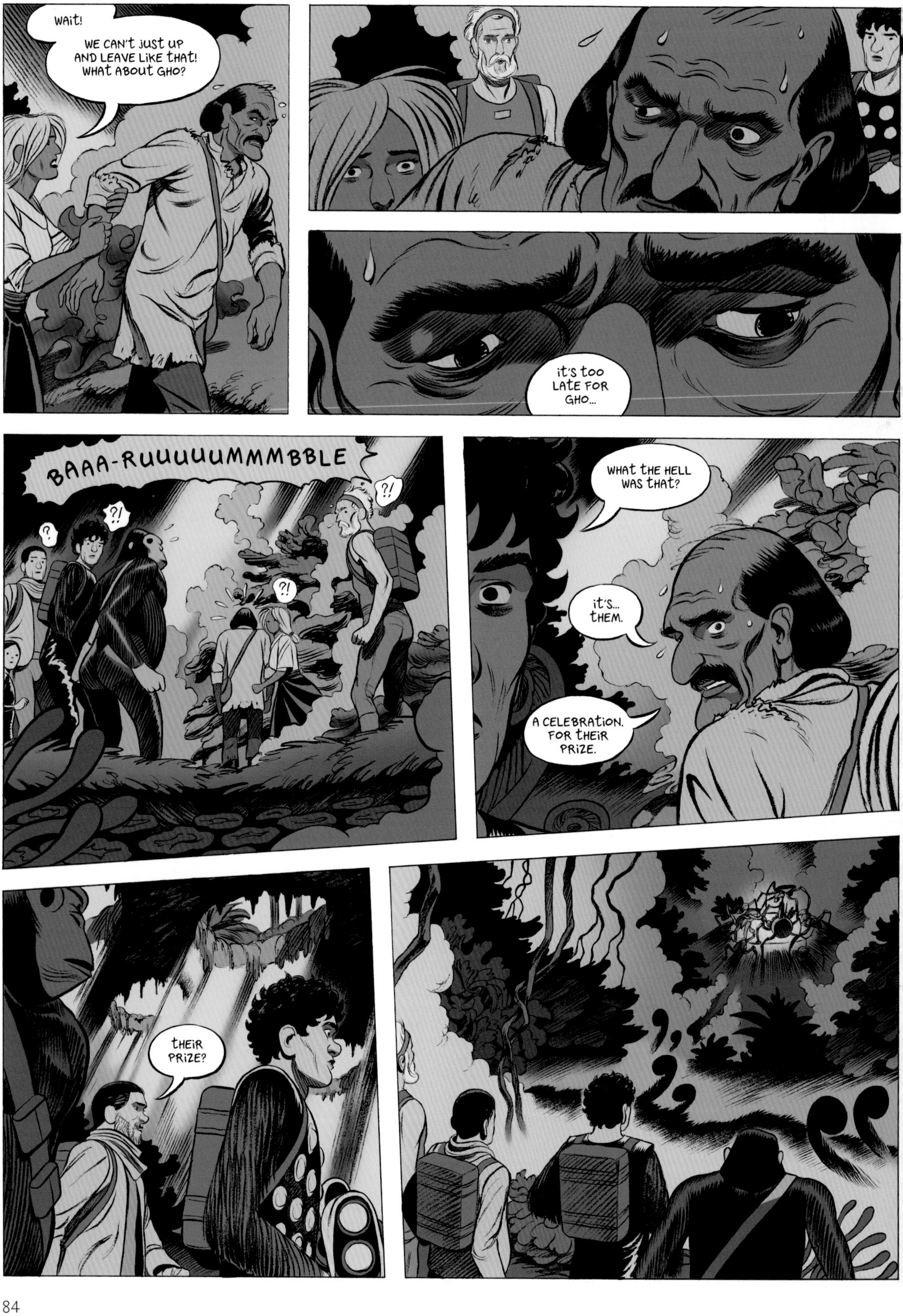
WAIT!
WE CAN'T JUST UP AND LEAVE LIKE THAT! WHAT ABOUT GHO?
IT'S TOO LATE FOR GHO...
BAAA-RUUUUUMMMBBLE
?
?!
?!
?!
WHAT THE HELL WAS THAT?
IT'S... THEM.
A CELEBRATION. FOR THEIR PRIZE.
THEIR PRIZE?

i CAN'T SEE A THING!

CAN ANYONE SEE ANYTHING?

CHURCHILL...

BINOCS.

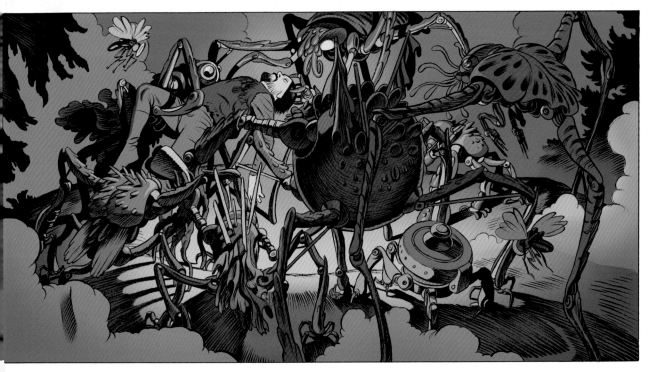

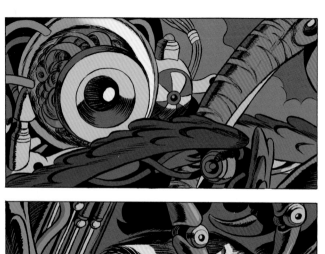
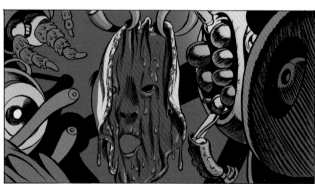

to be continued...